Never A
Dull Moment

Also by Peggy Holmes

IT COULD HAVE BEEN WORSE
(with Joy Roberts)

Never A Dull Moment

PEGGY HOLMES

with ANDREA SPALDING

COLLINS
TORONTO

First published 1984
by Collins Publishers
100 Lesmill Road, Don Mills, Ontario

Canadian Cataloguing in Publication Data

Holmes, Peggy, 1898 —
  Never a dull moment

ISBN 0-00-217277-1

1. Holmes, Peggy, 1898 —   2. Edmonton (Alta.) —
Biography.   I. Spalding, Andrea.   II. Title.

FC3696.26.H64A36 1984   971.23′3′00994   C84-098136-8
F1079.5.E3H64 1984

Printed and bound in Canada by John Deyell Company

*Dedicated to
my family,
my adopted families,
and many fine friends.
Each contributed,
in their own way,
to the colorful mosaic
of my life.*

Contents

Acknowledgements

Foreword

1	Looking Back	1
2	Things That Go Bump In The Night	6
3	Money Troubles	13
4	Bridging The Gap	17
5	Blow Outs And Break-ups	21
6	Crime Does Pay	26
7	Moving Up In The World	30
8	My Guardian Angel	35
9	Nipples, Nuts And Bolts	39
10	The Great Trans-Foothills Expedition	44
11	Holmes On The Trail	48
12	Business Dealings	53
13	Good Times	59
14	Rocky Road To Vancouver	64
15	High Society, Edmonton Style	70
16	Hitting The High Notes	75
17	An Interesting Condition	79

18	Being "Done" Right	85
19	Nine Days	91
20	England, Their England	96
21	Visitors	102
22	Moving To Vancouver	107
23	Taking Up Residence	112
24	Remuddling!	117
25	Deadline For Departure	121
26	Nightmare Ride	126
27	The Return	130
28	War Efforts	134
29	Giving A Leg Up	140
30	A Case of Forgery	144
31	From The Ridiculous To The Sublime	150
32	Retirement	154
33	Stick 'Em Up	161
34	The State Of The Art	165
35	In My Own Write	171
36	On My Own	177
37	The Bull And I	184

Illustrations between pages 112-113 and 144-145

Acknowledgements

I never thought I would retire my antique Underwood typewriter in favor of a computer at the Spaldings!

My thanks to Andrea, my co-author, with whom I spent many happy hours. Also her husband, David Spalding who patiently edited, and joined in our laughter and tears. Their love, understanding and many kindnesses went beyond the call of duty.

Thanks also to Margaret Paull who has supported me through two publications with Collins, and to Mary Riskin from the Writers Guild of Alberta, who gave moral support and advice.

I would also like to thank Alberta Culture for its helpful grant.

PEGGY HOLMES

David and I landed at Edmonton Airport in October 1967, typical raw English immigrants, very unsure of ourselves.

One week later we were introduced to Peggy and Harry Holmes and were instantly adopted by them. Peggy and Harry became the focus of our new life. They provided unstinting support, love, laughter and companionship and helped us adjust to the Canadian way of life.

I never dreamed that, sixteen years later, I would be a dyed-in-the-wool Albertan writing a book with the eminent broadcaster Peggy Holmes.

Working with Peggy is not only an honor but a labor of love, and I look forward with delight to many more joint ventures.

ANDREA SPALDING

Foreword

Never a Dull Moment by Peggy Holmes is a refreshing account of early Edmonton, and of the colourful personalities which have shaped the city and enriched our province. Told with an entertaining wit and optimism, the story unfolds Peggy's struggles against many obstacles and, in true pioneer spirit, her determination to overcome.

We are fortunate that Peggy Holmes recalls her life experiences with such flourish and enthusiasm: Her memory is indeed thorough. She depicts those seemingly hair-raising experiences which in hindsight are touching and amusing. We have witnessed in this century such tremendous changes, tremendous disappointments and struggles and also wonderfully happy times, good times. Peggy Holmes has been candidly generous to share with us not only the spirit of these early times, but the cherished and sweet memories of her life and loved ones.

I am sure you will enjoy this lively chronicle! For you it may also stimulate a whole wealth of memories of our early days as a province, and as a community of close networks and enduring friendships.

PETER LOUGHEED

Never A
Dull Moment

1
Looking Back

"Happy birthday, Papa!" "Happy birthday, Dad!"

The cheery voices of our son Bryan and his family burst in on our morning coffee, and well and truly woke us up.

Harry, my husband, was eighty-two. We hadn't given much thought to the actual birthday celebration, for when you reach our age you are just delighted that the birthdays keep rolling around.

Bryan, however, had other ideas.

"It's a beautiful day. How about a quick drive up to the old homestead you left forty-eight years ago. We've never seen it, you know."

Bryan had wanted to surprise us, and he certainly succeeded. I had never been so shocked in all my life.

"For heaven's sake," I gasped. "You can't just dash off like that! Our homestead is in the north country."

He laughed. "Nonsense, Mum! We'll have lunch on the way, and be home in time for dinner."

Harry was clearly moved at the thought of going back to "The Gables," the two-storey log house we had built in northern Alberta in 1920. He dearly loved that land he had "proved up" so many eons ago. All I felt was bewilderment. I wasn't so sure I wanted to return to the scene of so many hardships and disasters. Our homesteading days were a long time off, and I was quite content to leave things that way.

I heaved a quiet sigh. Everyone was so eager; how could I refuse to go?

The family excitedly helped us gather our supplies for the jaunt. It was difficult to comprehend that a pleasant day's trip in a shiny white Chrysler could accomplish what had been a major expedition forty-eight years earlier; why, it had taken us three days to get out then. Two days bouncing on the springless wagon seat along rutted, muddy trails, and one day's tedious train journey from the head of steel at Ashmont, into Edmonton.

I was very quiet in the car. Harry sat in front, animatedly answering eager questions from Cheryl and Brenda, our granddaughters. I hoped he wouldn't be disappointed. After all these years there may be nothing left to see.

The city was soon far behind, and we found ourselves barrelling through the country with its array of tailored farms. Gradually the farms became sparser and were interspersed with groves of aspen. I have always loved aspen trees with their trembling light green leaves. I'd watched them in fascination on the homestead. It took only the slightest breath of wind to set them dancing. They were such happy trees.

As we moved northward the aspens became denser, and there were great stretches of wooded bush with only intermittent farms. Then came the dark green of the spruce trees, the first sign of the great northern forests. We were nearly there.

Shortly before lunch we arrived in St. Lina, the town nearest our land. What a shock! I'd expected to see a modern version of the bustling little hamlet we had called civilization, but instead we found a ghost town.

Vanished were the houses, stables, rooming house and hotel that I had loved to see on our intermittent trips for supplies. My heart sank as I surveyed all that was left: a dilapidated store, the church and the skeletal remains of the post office. It looked so pitifully incongruous beside the modern highway.

To my relief, Harry persuaded Bryan it would be a good idea to have lunch not in the depressing remains of St. Lina, but at the Beaver River Crossing close to our homestead. The children thought a picnic by a river sounded fun, and only I knew that Harry had a hidden reason for his choice. What he really wanted to see was the spanking new bridge put up to replace the old wooden one he and his buddies had built before World War I.

It was nearly sixty years earlier that the Alberta Government first decided a crossing was needed over the Beaver River. In those days there was no province-wide road building and maintenance department to call upon, so local men were hired to do the work.

Harry and his friends spent many exhausting days hauling

logs from the bush so the contractor could build a sturdy bridge.

There was no room for weaklings in young Alberta. One time, the load that Harry and his friend Arthur Kilford were hauling rolled off the runners, pinning Arthur to the ground. The closest doctor was thirty miles away, and Harry could rely only on himself and his buddies as rescue team and medical help. Luckily, Arthur was only badly bruised; the boys managed to nurse him back to health.

That bridge caused so much blood, sweat and tears before it was completed. Imagine the disgust of the men when, fighting in far-off Flanders Fields, they had news from home telling them that it had sailed away with the ice blocks in the spring flood waters. So much for manpower!

It took many years, and much government money, concrete, and steel, to beat those floods and break-ups. The modern bridge delighted Harry — he was as proud of it as if he'd built it himself. We picnicked in its shade.

The picnic was only a brief reprieve. All too soon Bryan hustled us back into the car and we set off on the final leg of our journey to confront our dubious past. From now on Bryan had to follow Harry's directions.

The overgrown bush stretched around us in all directions, and to me it looked utterly unfamiliar. I'll never know how after all those years Harry knew where to turn, but he found the sagging gate like a homing pigeon. There, still faintly visible in the top plank, was the address "62-10-4 West of the Fourth meridian, The Gables."

Incredibly, I felt dissociated from the whole scene. I couldn't relate to my past. Had we really been that young couple who'd "gone up north" with stars in their eyes? Like so many other pioneers, we would leave those dreams in an abandoned cabin. I dimly remembered the interminable trip into the city with a sick father, and a few belongings piled behind us in a wagon. That old wagon had creaked with despair, all the way to the railroad.

Suddenly rising in front of us was the house. My heart gave a jump. We must have done something right, for it was still standing. The gables that had named it jutted out proudly, and even the shingles were on the roof. Admittedly it was minus its doors and windows, but there it stood — a firmly rooted, sightless old man, refusing to give up to the ghosts of the past.

The grandchildren were ecstatic. They leapt out of our car and dodged in and out of the doors and windows shrieking with glee at each new discovery. Brenda re-appeared, hanging out of the sagging kitchen window frame. With awe in her voice she asked, "Nana, did you really cook on this old stove?"

The memories came flooding back and I burst out laughing. Not only had I cooked on the darn thing, but during the freeze-up the chickens roosted along the top. One silly old hen insisted on laying her eggs there, while from the top of the kitchen dresser the rooster acted as our alarm clock.

Treading gingerly on the rotting floorboards, I entered my old kitchen. Someone obviously had used it as a cattle and feed shelter, and our footsteps stirred up chaff and straw. It was smelly, dark and dangerous, nothing like the cosy home of my memories.

The family scampered around upstairs, but Harry and I stood for a minute at the gaping window. I'd often gazed at the road from here, wistfully hoping for visitors who never came. Now the trail couldn't be seen. Forty-eight years' growth of poplar trees had sprung up to show nature's contempt for mere mortals.

As the tears rolled down my cheeks I tucked my arm through Harry's. "We're so lucky to have survived it all and end up with such a joyous family," I whispered.

Harry cocked his head to listen to the footsteps pounding upstairs. "Let's hope we survive a little longer," he grinned. "The rotting wood is liable to let our joyous family descend on our heads."

So we carefully helped each other out into the sunshine.

The girls emerged and went leaping over the tangled under-brush, crowing with delight when they found the remains of the barn. What a sorry sight. The walls had caved in and the sod roof had disintegrated. It was hard to imagine the rubble as the cosy place we had milked the cows, often at forty below zero, when our breath and the warm milk steamed into the frigid air. Only part of one wall remained, and that because it was propped up by the funny little three-cornered outside toilet I'd built for my father.

Rummaging in the rubble, Harry found the old walking plough and initiated Bryan into the mystery of straight furrows. Then I made my big discovery: the fence I'd built round the pig pen was still standing. Mind you, I'd built it to last. Harry had laughed at my use of great slabs of wood instead of normal lumber, and he was furious when he discovered I'd used a whole keg of precious six-inch spikes to hold them together. But it had survived, as I knew it would. It certainly had outlived the pigs, and the way those spikes were holding I'd no doubt it would outlive us.

Most of the farm equipment had been sold at the time of our hurried departure, when we rushed to get my father to a doctor in the city. But the remains of my old crock dash churn were unearthed, and the story of once finding a dead mouse in the cream had to be retold.

I was glad I'd outlived that old churn. In those days it was my master. I spent all my time bent over it. I would work and dash and paddle and mould what I thought was lovely-looking butter. Then I would hitch up the horses and drive five miles to the general store. I was so hopeful, but the reaction to my labors was always the same. The storekeeper would gingerly unwrap my butter, stick his nose in it, give a good hearty sniff, then surface shaking his head.

"Sorry, this is only third-rate butter. I can't give you anything for it. The grade one butter only sells for fifteen cents a pound."

Sadly I would rewrap my offering and drive back to the homestead. Come to think of it, the only thing the storekeeper ever bought was my eggs. It's hard to take credit for eggs! Maybe the roost over the cook stove added a subtle flavor.

Stumbling through the tangled grass that I had once proudly christened the "croquet lawn," I almost fell over the well, still safely boarded over as Harry had left it. Cheryl and Brenda found it really difficult to imagine that Harry and I had dug every inch of it ourselves. I'd no difficulty whatsoever remembering that episode. Just looking at it made my back ache.

The afternoon drew to a close and we took our seats in the well-upholstered car, ready for the return journey. Coming back had not been so painful after all. As Bryan closed the gate and settled behind the wheel, I mentally bid another farewell, this time to our old team of horses. Because of their half-starved appearance we'd laughingly named them Skin and Grief. They'd worked for us all the time we were homesteading. Uncomplainingly, they'd dragged us up and down the thirty-mile trail of pot holes and mud puddles where now we were driving so effortlessly on a well-paved highway. I hoped there was a horses' heaven. Skin and Grief certainly deserved the smooth green pastures they never experienced on our land.

As we sped smoothly down the highway toward Edmonton I dozed off, wondering why we hadn't returned to the homestead before. Possibly it was because Harry had said, "I never look back."

2
Things That Go
Bump In The Night

The city of Edmonton had never seemed so beautiful as it did driving home that night. Magically floating on a heat haze, the towering skyscrapers shone gold and orange, reflecting the setting sun.

I feasted my eyes. Who would have thought that this pleasant and airy city could spring from the dust and mud of the prairies?

The ethereal view contrasted vividly with my memories of the Edmonton of the twenties. In my sleepy state, instead of the aroma of warm upholstery from a new car I seemed to smell again the pungent fumes of the old-fashioned railway train, our last conveyance from the homestead.

The floodgates were unleashed and memories came pouring back: the nauseous rocking of the railroad car and the jostling of human bodies; the sounds of frightened cattle crammed together in the freight car behind us; the ensuing chaos at each station on the way, when stock and people were all unloaded at the same time.

I hated "mixed-goods trains" and their protesting smells, squeals and screams. It had been the final indignity of our traumatic journey back to so-called civilization, and I realized why I had supressed the memories for so long.

Despite the hardships we'd had some good times together on our western Canadian homestead. The Englishman's dream of land of his own so nearly came true for us. Unfortunately, fate changed the course of our lives when my father, in a desperate effort to regain his health in the clean air of Canada, was sent out to join us for a prolonged stay.

No one in England had comprehended the rigors we took in our stride. It was madness to send a sick man out to a northern outpost with no doctor within thirty miles, but by the time my mother's letter reached us my father had started his journey.

For the first few months Dad was with us, he seemed to improve and we hoped our fears were groundless. But the rigors of our lifestyle eventually took their toll, and by the end of the summer we knew we had been beaten.

Dad began having frequent blackouts. When these started they were a few minutes in length, but they gradually grew more serious until sometimes he was in a coma for several days. Our small capital did not allow the luxury of doctors and we tried to cope alone, but eventually we were forced to call Dr. Schoff, the old "doc" at Beaver River. Shaking his head he confessed there was nothing he could do. We must get my father to someone in the city as soon as possible.

We struggled on, hoping we would not have to give up our land which every day grew dearer to us. But someone had to keep an eye on father all the time, and my share of the work piled up. Then I found out I was pregnant.

That did it!

I'd lost a child once, and Harry had no intention of letting me lose this one for lack of help. He made an instant decision, and with tears rolling down my cheeks, I started packing.

7

We looked like a travelling circus when, in 1923, we arrived in Edmonton. Harry as ringmaster jumped off the train, his regular dapper self, then proceeded to hand out of the carriage my father, who weaved to and fro on the verge of passing out. I appeared next, pregnant, travel-sick, and covered with train smuts from hanging my face out the open window in an effort to get fresh air. Buster our dog trotted out with his plumed tail wagging. He was pleased as punch with the whole experience and managed to get in everyone's way.

Trying to unload our immediate possessions was a centre-ring act. As people grabbed at the series of badly wrapped parcels that had travelled with us, bits dropped out. I never could wrap a parcel neatly at the best of times. Trying to do the job in a hurry while looking after my father had been beyond me. Buster galloped around retrieving things, thinking this was a new game, while the station personnel swore at him and I tried to pretend he didn't belong to us.

I remember standing on the station platform doggedly hanging on to Buster with one hand and my father with the other. We were surrounded by untidy debris, the remains of our home, and I was desperately tired. Harry, waving his arms and talking earnestly, persuaded the train officials to find a corner where we could store our furniture until we located a house. While they foraged around I tried to pull myself together in case my father had one of his periodic blackouts.

Having no idea where we were going or how we would get there, I eyed the hard wooden benches in the waiting room. We just might be sleeping on those.

Harry had written to a friend, warning him we were coming to the city. Unfortunately, we had not been able to give him a date. How could we? We needed time to sell or give away the livestock, and also to wait for my father to get over one of his attacks so that he could travel.

All the other people at the station seemed to know where they were going and what they were doing. I resentfully eyed the bustling crowd and suddenly saw a face I knew. Coming toward us, wearing the friendliest, most welcoming smile I had ever seen, was Jimmy Dunstall, Harry's friend.

8

Jimmy was kindness itself — he had been meeting the train every day. He whisked us off to his house and said we could stay there until we found a place of our own. I burst into tears.

At this point in my life I was feeling completely overwhelmed. Preoccupied by my new pregnancy after losing the previous baby, I was also very worried about my father and his mysterious disease.

It's funny how when you are really distressed, the most simple thing can seem like a miracle, and Jimmy made a miracle happen for me. He showed us into his house, and I found myself confronted with a real bathtub.

Hardly daring to believe my eyes, I tentatively turned the tap. Hot water gushed forth. Heaven! No more filling iron pots and boiling water on the stove. I filled the tub to the brim, lowered myself in and did not stir for an hour. As the steam rose so did my spirits. Maybe Edmonton was not such a bad place after all.

By today's standards, the Edmonton of the twenties left a lot to be desired. Situated above the winding North Saskatchewan River, its most imposing building was the MacDonald Hotel.

Visitors gasped in amazement at this incongruous edifice stuck in the middle of the plains. Built in the style of a French chateau, it gazed haughtily across the river valley, stonily ignoring the mud streets, wooden sidewalks and false fronts that lined the rest of the wide trail so hopefully called Jasper Avenue. The only other structure to compete with its grandeur was the Legislature Building with its gleaming dome, at the other end of town.

Edmonton was a dirty city, with clouds of dust stirred up by the passing streetcars, horse-drawn wagons, and the encroaching new-fangled motor cars. But after life in the homestead, Jimmy's small clapboard house with electricity and running water seemed like Buckingham Palace.

Our most urgent needs, permanent accommodation and a doctor, seemed modest but proved almost impossible to meet. All our money was tied up in the homestead and its land. Right now we hadn't a penny to fly with.

Harry, undaunted, applied the hunting skills learned in the bush to hunting for a house, and arrived back triumphant the first day out. He had rented the top half of a two-storey house, newly

9

decorated and incredibly cheap at fifteen dollars a month. So scared was he that it would be snapped up, he had signed on the spot a lease for one year.

I was thankful to get into a permanent home so quickly, and with an address we could cable my mother in England: "Come out quick. Help look after Father." Things began to look as though they were getting organized.

The house was terrific. The walls had been coated with spanking white calcimine paint, and I quickly hung up my bright cretonne curtains. Harry gathered the rest of our furniture from the station, and we spent the day arranging our few basic belongings. By evening we had a cheerful new home.

I organized our English china carefully on the kitchen dresser, spread our beautiful satin eiderdown on our bed and turned down the sheets. Dad seemed happy with a camp bed set up in the other bedroom, and so, after a hectic day, we prepared to turn in. Harry and I hit our pillows with a sigh of relief, and sleep came very quickly.

In the early hours I woke up with a start. *Something was biting me.* Never being one to suffer alone in silence I sat bolt upright and let out a piercing scream.

Harry sprang up quite annoyed.

"What in heaven's name is the matter now?"

He switched on the light, and a troop of bedbugs scampered up the wall.

This was catastrophic. I'd battled all kinds of animals on the farm, but I refused to cohabit with bedbugs. I was not going to sleep in that bed.

Finally Harry coaxed me into sitting in a comfortable chair in the kitchen, near Buster. I kept the light on and dozed fitfully for the remainder of the night.

No wonder the rent was so cheap. We should have smelled trouble from the first. The landlord was quite hostile and refused to let us out of the lease. Having no money we were faced with staying in that buggy apartment until Mother arrived from England, and for many endless nights I slept in the kitchen chair with the light on.

Finally, after a month of this, Mother arrived. Father was ill again, so I had to look after him while Harry went to meet her at the station. I sent him off with strict instructions to prepare Mother for the state we were in. Imagine my surprise when in a very short time they arrived not on the streetcar, but driving up to the door in a large open automobile.

On the boat to Canada, Mother had met some wealthy business people from Edmonton. She always made friends easily, and in no time at all they were bosom pals. They had travelled together on the train to Edmonton, and naturally they offered to run her home. She waved them off in a flurry of goodbyes and promises to entertain them in return. I was frozen with horror.

Mother looked the picture of quiet elegance. She sat gracefully on our chair with her squirrel wrap trailing on the floor behind her. Always the talkative sort, she burbled happily about the wonderful friends she had met on the sea voyage and the adventures she'd had. She was full of the visits she hoped to make now she was in Canada at last.

Naturally, she hadn't a clue as to the dilemma we were in. As I listened to her I kept hoping the bugs weren't rooting around in her fur.

Dad was very quiet, listening to her chatter. Suddenly he turned to me and dropped his bombshell.

"I can't sleep with her. All that talking will drive me crazy. Did she always chatter like that?"

Help! Here we were in a two-bedroom apartment. Harry refused to sleep with me in the kitchen, and now my father was refusing to sleep with my mother. Well, they didn't have any choice, and I bedded them down together, praying that miraculously the bedbugs would not strike.

The miracle did not happen, and it only took my mother about half an hour to size up the situation. The morning couldn't come fast enough. As soon as it was light she had Harry out of the door looking for a new place to live, and she tackled the landlord.

The landlord was not prepared for my mother. He was used to dealing with me, and we were in no position to argue. Mother was made of sterner stuff. The more he yelled and blustered and threatened to sue us, the more ladylike but determined she became. When she started asking questions about Edmonton's health department, he retired rapidly.

I never did find out what finally transpired between them; I was too mortified by the whole situation.

I had told Harry I didn't care what kind of hovel he found so long as it was clean, and once again he came in with good news. He'd found a place down by the river on Ross Flats.

Ross Flats was a very pleasant area of the city but, built on the Saskatchewan River's flood plain, it continually had vacancies. The house he found was built of awful concrete blocks and was the only building in the area to have survived the devastating flood of 1915. In the spring of that year the melt water had rushed across the flood plain, carrying all the houses and barns in the area off downstream and leaving this concrete house standing alone amid a scene of total devastation. Now it stood in a lordly position, gazing arrogantly at the raw-looking new buildings going up around it.

I was impatient.

"Never mind floods, how about bugs?"

Harry had talked to the next-door neighbor, who had assured him it was clean. She seemed very kind, and Harry told me he thought we would have a good friend there. How right he was. The MacOwen family was truly wonderful.

The next move was hard and costly. Everything we owned was sent to be cleaned and fumigated before being delivered to the concrete house.

Thank goodness Mother had brought some cash with her. We were able to spend three days in a hotel while everything was dealt with. Those were the most expensive bedbugs in Edmonton.

At last, with clean carpets, draperies and bedding, we were able to settle in. I fell in love with our ugly old house and christened it The Concrete Castle. Our neighbor was correct; it was clean. Surrounded by large trees full of birds, and with a garden that ran down to the river's edge, our castle was a place where we could be happy. Mother took over and organized the move, and my spirits rose even though we had moved down to the flats.

3
Money Troubles

Our address on "the flats" was most appropriate, for we were flat broke. We had always been self-supporting on the homestead, where the key to survival was food — and we'd grown our own. In the city we found the key to survival was cash, the one commodity we couldn't grow.

Harry optimistically turned his skills to job hunting, but in 1923 times were hard and jobs few. There wasn't much call for his odd set of skills. After all, who wanted to hire a champion roller-skater or ex-farmer/soldier? Luckily he did have a diploma for writing Pitman's shorthand, but even this didn't seem to do any good. Jobs were just not available.

The Ross Flats were, in theory, not far from the downtown area. We could see the city buildings perched on the edge of the river valley overlooking us. In actuality it was quite difficult to get up there. A tram regularly trundled up the cliff, but in order to save even the streetcar fare, Harry usually climbed the 232 steps up the almost vertical hillside. These steps eventually brought him out, winded but in reach of the MacDonald Hotel and the centre of Edmonton. He might be out of work but he was certainly physically fit.

Pregnancy and lack of energy confined me to the concrete castle. Every day I watched Harry cheerfully stride off up the hill. Each evening his returning steps seemed slower and slower. He never needed to tell me he was still jobless; his whole body showed dejection. Our meals shrank to the middle of the plate as our finances dwindled. Even Mother's little nest-egg began to disappear. The approach of rent-day became a nightmare.

One day Harry arrived home and was surprised to find me beaming. I'd some good news for a change. Our neighbor from the homestead, Ole Neilson, had rounded up our range cattle and shipped them into town with his own. Ole had called in to tell me he was taking our cattle to Gainer's Packing Plant and would be back later with the cheque.

We spent a most happy evening speculating on how much the cattle would fetch. After all we had several animals including Daisy, our lovely little milk cow. She'd originally cost us $125. With her value added to that the range cattle might bring we should be able to pay the rent, give Mother back her nest-egg, and fill the larder.

Imagine our dismay when the cheque arrived. Not only was it pitifully small, but our Daisy was listed as fit only for the cutting and canning department, and her portion of the cheque was sixty cents. I've never been able to enjoy a hot dog since.

Thank goodness for our next door neighbor. Mrs. MacOwen came over every day with vegetables from her garden and bouquets of beautiful flowers. I became a whiz at vegetarian cookery, and my mother learned not to sniff at dandelion salad. We didn't have much meat on the table, but the beautiful floral arrangements were worthy of the best hotel in town.

Over the years I have many times blessed our good friends. In this time of need, while the MacOwen family was making sure we didn't starve, Bob and Emily Andison came to our rescue with the offer of a job.

We first met the Andisons when Emily's brother served with Harry in the first world war. Harry and I were welcomed into their family and we became good friends. I missed them when we moved to the homestead, and we were very happy to renew our friendship following our return to the city.

We were most impressed to find Bob had become Clerk of the Legislative Assembly, and were even more amazed when he suddenly appeared at our door and asked Harry if he would care to be his secretary for one month.

Needless to say, Harry was only too delighted, particularly when he heard the salary for that period was to be seventy-five dollars. Bob's secretary was off on a month's holiday. Harry and I wished her bon voyage; in fact, we wished she would have such a good time she wouldn't want to return.

Seventy-five dollars was a real windfall for us. It covered our rent, utilities and food, and gave us a little more time to catch our breath. We hoped that a permanent job would turn up before the month ran out. We were even within walking distance of the Legislature Building, for it sat upstream from us on the site of the original Fort Edmonton. Once again Harry could save tram fare.

Pounding the city's streets each day had allowed Harry to become familiar with its ways very quickly. With his ear to the ground and his nose for a good bargain he often shopped for me, picking up reduced prices on items that would not keep. It was thus that we heard about Queen City Meat Market.

Meat was a problem in those days of poor refrigeration. The butchers could not keep it over the weekend, so anything left in the meat market by Saturday evening was sold off cheaply. Queen City Meats, however, had no ordinary cut-price sale. Mr. Noak, the colorful owner, had a real flair for business. He ran a full-scale auction.

Every Saturday evening, about five, people started to gather. Suddenly Noak would appear like magic, head and shoulders above the crowd as he jumped on a bench, and with a stentorian bellow call us all to attention. Then the bidding started raging. Christie's Auction House had nothing on us except the price; we were bidding in cents.

Soon it was over, and many happy people left carrying beautiful beef roasts for less than a dollar. Those who were unlucky shrugged and promised to return the following week. I wonder if Noak ever realized what a service he was supplying to those of us in straitened circumstances. That Saturday roast often had to last us the week. Luckily, I'd performed wonders with rabbit on the homestead, and what I could do with a small roast of beef was magical.

With the necessities of life taken care of, we turned our attention to finding a doctor for my father. A friend recommended one in the McLeod Building, a majestic three-story brick edifice halfway down Jasper Avenue. We were suitably impressed. Anyone with an office there must be good. Little did I know that many years later our future son, Bryan, would marry into the McLeod family. By that time, however, this once tall building would be dwarfed by a jungle of high-rises.

The doctor obviously belonged with the building. He was an imposing medic of the Victorian era with a watch chain over his well-developed stomach, and eyeglasses perched on the end of his nose. He looked as though he were about to burst with his own importance, though I later realized he was bursting with inefficiency. He diagnosed Dad's trouble easily, but could offer no suggestions for dealing with it.

"Dangerously high blood pressure, I don't know how he's survived the trip in from the homestead. He could die any minute."

And that was the extent of his doctoring. Telling us there was no medicine for high blood pressure, he dismissed us.

Harry persisted. "Surely there is something that can be done?"

The doctor shrugged, "Well I suppose you could try and diet him. No red meat, salt, alcohol. But you might as well not bother. He won't stick to that diet; his sort never do."

Poor old Dad. His face got glummer and glummer as he listened to this rude man talk as if he weren't there. Dad was a Yorkshire man who loved his roast beef, Yorkshire pudding, roast potatoes, and of course his beer. He silently got up and walked out. As we followed, the doctor had a parting shot.

"He's going to die anyway. It's your wife you should be looking after."

My pregnancy was obviously showing, and because we didn't know any other doctor we thought we'd better ask this one to look after me.

We never discussed the doctor's diagnosis with Father, but that night we placed before him not the usual meat dish but a poached egg on spinach, followed by stewed prunes. He didn't protest. Mother soon took over the menu planning and followed the doctor's instructions to the letter. Dad successfully lived on that diet for the next fifteen years.

4
Bridging The Gap

The end of Harry's clerical work came all too quickly, and once again I was worrying about what we would do at the end of the month. Racking our brains for a solution to our cash problems, we went for a walk.

A walk with Harry was always a slightly irritating experience. I'd waddle along looking at the birds, trees and the world in general. Harry always strolled very sedately, with his head down and his hands behind his back, royal family style. He never seemed to glance at the world around him, yet he missed nothing. He always managed to point out something I'd overlooked. Infuriating!

This evening Harry suddenly stopped, bent down and picked up a dirty piece of metal. He handed it to me, casually remarking. "That's bridge work from someone's teeth." I was not impressed, but Harry insisted on taking it home and washing it. Despite this attention it still looked to me like a tatty piece of bent metal, and I certainly missed the point: that dentists in those days only worked in gold.

The following morning Harry solemnly donned his one suit and strolled sedately into Birks, the classy jewellers. With the dignity of one parting with the family heirlooms, he proceeded to sell them the gold bridge.

I wish I could recollect how much it brought us, but I only know it saved the day. I do remember gasping in astonishment at Harry's gall. Heavens, if we'd invested that gold in the bank we could have bought an apartment block today.

Once again Bob Andison proved to be a good Samaritan. A vacancy for a court reporter was advertised at the police courts. Bob rushed by and advised Harry to apply quickly.

Harry hesitated. It was years since he had learned shorthand, mainly for a dare. His speed was slow and the idea of having to keep pace with verbal evidence seemed overwhelming. Besides, he was sure he would never pass the entrance exams.

"Try it, lad. You've a whole week to brush up your shorthand speeds. Peggy will help you." Bob looked at me encouragingly.

As far as I was concerned it was a terrific idea. I nodded furiously. Besides, anyone who turned down Harry for a job couldn't see past his nose. I was sure his quiet dignity would grace any courtroom. Excitedly I pressed Bob for more details.

If successful, Harry would qualify for the married man's salary of one hundred and twenty-five dollars per month, plus commission. Riches indeed! I was puzzled, though; what on earth was "plus commission"? I envisaged Harry, resplendent in commissionaire's uniform, standing at a courtroom door graciously accepting tips as people filed in. Reality was a lot less glamorous. It transpired that the court reporter made a verbatim copy of the case for the court files, but copies the lawyers needed were purchased from the court reporter. This was the commission.

Mother and I were determined that Harry should be a successful applicant for the job. We became his "readers" and read aloud from every book we could lay hands on. Harry scribbled away in shorthand, trying desperately not to miss a syllable we uttered. Never have I had such interest in my every word.

In an effort to make things more interesting for all, I varied his literary diet from the Bible to True Confessions. I hoped the latter would give him practice for the seamier side of life.

Dad, who couldn't take this constant chatter, had one of his periodic blackouts for a couple of days. He needed to get away from it all.

Thank goodness our endeavours were successful, and Harry passed the test with flying colors. (We found out later he'd been the only applicant.) We promised ourselves a real celebration when the first paycheque arrived. I looked forward to visiting the Rialto movie theatre where for the price of a ticket you not only saw the film but were given a dinner plate. For now, however, we contentedly mounted the steps to the city and splurged on a five cent cup of coffee at the American Dairy Lunch, the "in" gathering place of Edmonton.

The restaurant was underground, and we sat below a roof of great glass slabs that acted as the sidewalk for the pedestrians

18

above. Drinking our coffee, we watched the distorted feet through the glass and listened to a tiny fountain play over flaccid-looking goldfish. This, in conjunction with the hideous gargoyles around the walls, was considered the height of fashion.

The excitement was obviously too much for me, as later that night I had a dreadful dream with gargoyles chasing me up and down the cliff steps. I woke up screaming and it took me a while to orient myself.

Once fully awake I was startled to find Harry in the middle of the room hurriedly pulling on his trousers.

"Heavens! Where are you going? It's the middle of the night."

He heaved a sigh of relief and shot quickly back into bed. "I was ready to take you to the hospital," he replied sleepily, "I thought you were in labor."

Being an optimist, I'd hoped most of our troubles were over now that Harry had a steady pay packet. Unfortunately we'd not realized how demanding his job would be, or that it would involve certain expenditures. First, we had to find more of that precious commodity, money, to buy him a typewriter. As we were so hard up, we arranged to buy it on the "glad or sorry system." We were glad to borrow the money, but sorry we had to pay it back with interest.

Harry was thrown in at the deep end with his first case, a very upsetting abortion scandal that caused a sensation in the press at that time. With six doctors throwing medical terms at him, he needed more money to buy a medical dictionary to help him spell them.

This dictionary became the first volume of a very extensive support library. Forty years later I used it for my own support, sitting squarely on it while I typed my scripts with the same second-hand Underwood we'd purchased for that first case.

Even now, as I sit working late at night, I seem to hear the echo of Harry's typing as he too labored into the early hours, transcribing the cases in time for the next morning.

It was unfortunate that Harry's first case was so unsavory. Sex and abortion were not discussed easily, and after losing our first child through a breech birth I didn't want to hear about such things. Poor Harry would struggle on his own late into the night disentangling his hieroglyphics. Evidently True Confessions had not been much use; it didn't contain enough long words.

I was very lonely. Harry immersed himself in the new job in a desperate endeavor to get the evidence transcribed on time. I couldn't go out. My pregnancy was showing, and pregnancy was kept very quiet then. One didn't parade it around proudly; instead, we scuttled into our houses like frightened rabbits.

Periodic visits to the doctor held no reassurance. He wasn't a gynecologist and all he did was listen to my heart. I attended no prenatal classes. Not that it bothered me; I'd never even heard of them. All I asked from the doctor was that he minister to me during the delivery. Other than these visits, I spent many weary days watching the river flowing past my window, heaving my growing bulk around our garden for a walk among the fall leaves, and talking to Buster.

Eventually on a cold November night I was admitted to the Royal Alexandra City Hospital. Can you imagine a hospital without resident doctors on duty? The hospital was full of nurses, but at that time it had no interns. My doctor was busy in his office.

It was a very prolonged birth. For two days and two nights I battled. At the end of that time I was exhausted and ready to die. The nurses did their best for me, but there was a limit to how much they were allowed to do.

Eventually, I remember, I buried my head in my pillow and pleaded to God to help me. He did. Our twin daughters were born just then, on the bed, and I passed out.

When I came to in the case room, the doctor appeared and broke the news to me that my twins were dead. "I couldn't have done anything," he blustered. "They've been dead for at least twenty-four hours."

Harry came in with my mother. He put his arms around me and laid his cheek comfortingly against mine. "We've still got each other," he whispered, but my arms ached for the little babies I'd never ever held, and all I could do was sob.

Mother tried to comfort me. While I had been in the hospital, my grandfather in England had died and left me some money. It would be arriving any day.

I bitterly turned my face to the wall.

"Yes, just in time to pay the doctor and the undertaker."

I never saw the doctor again.

More than a year later, when talking to a nurse who'd befriended me in those dreadful days, I heard the full truth of the story. "Such a pity those babies of yours died," she remarked. "They were alive at birth, and the nurses did their best to save them."

I was speechless.

5
Blow-outs
And Break-ups

Returning from the hospital to a tidy house, I found every tiny reminder of the expected babies had been spirited away. I wrapped myself in a mental cocoon and proceeded to "forget" the whole incident. In fact, I forgot most things. I just sat and sat, gazing at the frozen river.

Everything seemed grey to me at that time, the lowering sky, the unemployed men slowing walking up the frozen riverbank, the bare winter trees with their arms stretched beseechingly toward the sky. Even my parents seemed to move silently around in a grey fog.

People were very kind and endeavored to interest me in the happenings on the flats. Neighbors regularly popped in and out with baking and preserves, and Mrs. MacOwen came every day with news of interesting happenings. Truly, I did try to respond.

Watching the river turned out to be good therapy, for it was such a busy place. On the opposite bank, where there was a surface coal seam, young boys cut the coal out, loaded it up on sleighs and took it home to their families — a very welcome addition to the budget. Sad old men scratched around in the snow, picking up loose pieces and stuffing their pockets.

Where the river had overflowed and frozen solid and smooth, the ice skaters glided by in colorful toques, mitts and long flowing scarves. The frozen riverbank was a favorite place for weekend recreation.

The Arctic Ice Company worked near our house on the riverbank. Employees cut huge blocks of ice out of the river. These were sold to houses and shops around the city and stored in cold rooms for refrigeration.

Once, my friend Marion and her fiancé strolled past. They were gingerly walking around the unsafe blocks left by the ice company when the young man disappeared. He'd fallen into a hole covered by drifting snow. Marion had been an army nurse and was used to acting promptly in emergencies. She grabbed his coat with one hand, firm ice with the other, and yelled long and loud. She soon attracted a crowd, and her fiancé was dragged out safely.

Unfortunately the romance went cold. Marion found it hard to explain that the sight of him shivering and shrunken by her side had put her off for life. I have often wondered what would have happened if it had been the other way around and *he* had rescued *her*. Would she have fallen passionately in love with him, or would he have had the same reaction?

A neighbor's young son came one day with an exciting new discovery — radio. He made me a little crystal set that I thought was the cat's whiskers. This young genius first sized up our concrete castle. Then he decided the radio would work if one wire was attached to the springs of our bed and the other to the water tap in the kitchen. He proceeded to festoon his wires around, and we hoped for the best. I had always loved music and had been very frustrated on the homestead where we had only two records for our wind-up Gramophone — Knowest Thou the Land, and The Anvil Chorus. We played them so much I was heartily sick of them, and vowed I would never listen to them again.

The magic moment arrived. We crouched down together, our ears poised to catch the slightest sound. The young boy switched on and fiddled with a little knob. I couldn't believe my ears. Horrors! It was The Anvil Chorus.

Despite this inauspicious beginning, I really enjoyed that little crystal set. I listened to it by the hour and gradually it brought me in touch with the real world again. Our young friend made daily improvements, and eventually every one in the room could hear well as he fashioned us a speaker out of a Ford motor horn.

By Christmas time our circle of friends had grown. As Harry had earned extra money with his commissions, we could afford a few treats and even gave each other presents. It was a great improvement over our Christmas on the homestead. I wasn't feeling well enough to enjoy full-scale celebrating, but we did manage to have a family meal with my mother in charge of the turkey and Harry making a good approximation of a plum pudding. I enjoyed myself in a quiet way, and so just after Christmas we decided to invite a friend for lunch.

Aunt Jane was really no relation, but she'd helped us when I'd come to Canada four years earlier. Well, the fuss we made, you'd think it was royalty coming to call. Of course, in her own estimation, Aunt Jane was royal. She was an older lady with private means, never seen without her kid gloves.

I decided to serve a fish dish. Harry and I had been given a wedding gift of some beautiful fish knives and forks with matching servers, and this was a good chance to show them off. With our Royal Doulton dishes (the ones I had fed the hens from, on the homestead) and a snowy white tablecloth, we were all set.

The majority of houses in our area were heated by either a wood-burning or coal-burning stove. Our concrete castle was heated by an old pot-bellied Quebec heater that dominated the whole living area and gobbled up coal at a furious rate. Heaving coal into its open jaws and slamming the door shut on the resulting upheaval, always reminded me of a line from an old limerick: "Its rumblings internal were something infernal."

This day we stoked up as usual to get the house nice and warm for our guest. Then it happened! With an enormous roar, the Quebec heater in the living room blew out.

The stove pipes along the ceiling came apart at the joints and we spluttered and choked as soot filled the air. At that very

23

moment the taxi deposited Aunt Jane at the door, and there she stood, complete with white gloves.

"Goodness gracious! Whatever has happened?"

All I could do was to cough and splutter and point to the stove while the tears made grimy tracks down my cheeks.

She patted my shoulder. "Never mind, my deah. I always rise to the occasion." And, firmly placing her gift of potted preserves in the kitchen, she stripped off her gloves, rolled up her sleeves, and helped us clean up — all with great dignity.

Her dignity never left her. Years later, when she was dying, she summoned her nephew to her bedside and ordered him to go out and buy a bottle of champagne. "My family always die drinking champagne. I will await your return."

She did, and together they toasted her passing.

"The flats," as I had now learned to call them, were a very close-knit community in which the churches played a leading role. That year we were very glad of the support of the church. Not only was it solace for me when I was low, but it offered a variety of social occasions. Mother and Dad joined the bridge club, and had several cheerful nights out at the church enjoying various parties.

I was really staggered and extremely angry when, several years later, I met a deaconess from a church in England who informed me she was "going to work with the heathens on Ross Flats." My memories of the flats are not of heathens, but of very kindly people.

Flood stories ran rampant on the flats, especially toward the end of the winter. As the weather got warmer most Edmontonians began to look forward to the break-up. Not on the flats, however. Our people would wander down to the river bank and try to size up the amount of ice that had to melt and estimate how high up the river would come.

All the time we had been living there I had been told stories of the Great Flood, when the rush of water had been so fierce it had swept away almost all the buildings. The river surface was black with logs, animals, barns and houses. People were rescued from floating roofs and all their personal belongings bobbed away down the North Saskatchewan River.

24

Even the local brickyard was swept away, and the few houses that withstood the flood were awash to the second storey. For thirty-six hours the waters rose and rampaged through the area. Eventually the Low Level Bridge itself was in danger of being swept off as the angry water rose to within fourteen inches of its decking. In desperation a railway train was loaded with coal, driven on to the bridge and left to hold it down. This device worked, much to the relief of all concerned.

At that time Edmonton had a population of sixty thousand, and it was estimated that fifty thousand gathered anxiously on the upper banks to view this disastrous flood.

Understandably, anxiety about the spring break-up colored my thoughts, and every day I would walk to the edge of our garden and look at the river. The pressure from the ice slabs made them rear up on end in great pinnacles, the scene resembling a crazily iced cake. I'd look from the great floes to the bridge and wonder how it could possibly withstand the vicious strength of the ice, let alone the meltwaters. But despite my fears, as the temperature rose so did my spirits.

The roaring and cracking of the ice became incredible. You could hardly hear yourself speak. Lottery tickets were sold so people could bet both on the day and time of the actual break-up. My sleep became punctuated with nightmares of our being drowned in our beds, and I found myself listening for the creaks and groans of the ice. Each day a bigger crowd gathered on the banks to watch. Finally, under a blue sky and bright sun, the river gave a great roar and started to move again. An answering cheer went up from the waiting crowd and hats were thrown up in the air. Spring was truly on its way.

One cannot grieve forever. As the ice melted away my heart became lighter, and I was stronger in every way. My fears of flooding were assuaged and I could look forward at last to the months ahead.

I celebrated by jotting a few lines:
The ice floes
Passing the window
Carry away my grief.
The wild free birds fly north,

Budding trees herald the spring.
My tied down spirits break their bonds,
I can live again.

6
Crime Does Pay

Apart from Dad's blackouts, nothing untoward happened for the next few weeks. The blackouts we were getting used to. After all he only seemed to miss a couple of days and then bounce back as chipper as ever. Referring to them as "Dad's attacks," we'd make him comfortable in his bed and carry on with our daily duties until he surfaced. There was nothing else we could do.

Thank goodness Dad's disposition was basically jolly. It was amazing how rapidly after an attack he could function again. He loved Gilbert and Sullivan operettas and, on his good days, would recite them by the hour. Unfortunately he could not sing a note, not even the national anthem.

Mother, however, had hidden talents. She had been a noted whistler in her time, the star turn of several talent shows in her youth. To hear my dad reciting, and Mother whistling the tune in the background, was quite funny. There was certainly no need to buy a parrot or canary in our house. Occasionally Buster would raise his voice to join them, but you could tell his teachers had been the coyotes.

After toiling in the police courts for some weeks, Harry suggested I pay a visit so I could see his working situation. I'd imagined the seat of justice to be impressive and dignified; I couldn't have been more mistaken. The court was such an incredibly run-down old building that I thought I'd come to the wrong address. Rumor said it had once been an old Salvation Army hostel but the building had become so decrepit they had moved out. I believed it. The prison kitchen was on the main floor. To get to the courts I mounted a staircase that acted as flue for all the cooking smells of old stew and permanently boiling cabbage. It was nauseating.

Once in the courtroom you had to strain your ears to catch all that was said as the building was situated next to Number Two fire hall. Learned matters would be droning along, then suddenly bells would start ringing, horses snorting, and the old red fire engine would rattle past.

As I watched Harry bent over a desk scribbling frantically, I felt very sorry for him. At heart he was a man of the woods and here he was, trapped in this very demanding job. I was glad I had made the effort to go and see him at work. Understanding the conditions and pressures made me feel much more sympathetic toward him and less sorry for myself.

During that visit I made another friend, Old Sol. He was a badly handicapped and disfigured man who had been adopted by the firemen at the fire hall. In fact Old Sol was rumored to live at the fire hall, though everyone turned a blind eye to this. His terrible disfigurement was said to have been caused by an accident involving a horse. If this was so he seemed to bear no malice. He was devoted to the fire horses, and when a horse was upset it was Sol who calmed it down.

Sol sallied forth each day with a tray of cigarettes hanging from a leather belt around his neck. He had a list of steady customers and spent the day delivering the cigarettes they had ordered. He was a well-known city character, much beloved, and was to pop in and out of my life at regular intervals for the next fifteen years.

Now that I could visualize the courts I'd a renewed interest in Harry's job, and when he wasn't too exhausted he would tell me about some of the cases. One day he came in laughing.

"There I was, reading the charge of 'drunk and disorderly vagrant with no visible means of support,' when the old reprobate in the dock shouts out 'Hello Harry,' and gives me a big wave."

It was one of our friends from the homestead. Fortunately the judge was amused by this incident. If he had been in a bad mood it could have added to the fine. A few weeks later another acquaintance from the homestead was arrested. He was utterly awed by Harry's position and insisted on calling him "Yer Ludship."

The first few weeks at a new job are always hard. Harry came home from the police courts with blinding headaches, and how he persevered every night to transcribe the long complicated cases, I'll never know. For many weeks his spare time was spent dozing. The constant concentration on spoken and written words drained him more than any physical work on the farm. He couldn't even bear to be read to. His mind needed a complete rest.

Later he described those early days as a slice of Gilbert and Sullivan light opera. First he had to act as Clerk of the Court. After the magistrate, Colonel Primrose, was ushered in and seated on the bench (under the large oil painting of King George V), the Clerk of the Court — our Harry — had to read the docket and the charges to the prisoners. Then he changed hats and rushed around to his desk, ready to take notes.

All the rub-a-dubs and prostitutes who had been picked up overnight were dealt with one by one while Harry scribbled frantically to report each case verbatim. He was so thankful when a Chinese case was heard. An interpreter was needed and that slowed down the proceedings and allowed him to catch his breath.

Some aspects of the job were obviously very unpleasant, but what upset us most was the plight of the mental patients. In those days all mentally disturbed people had to be certified through the police courts. These tragic cases often spent the night in the prison cells, with their names on labels tied around their necks.

In the morning they were herded into the dock with the criminals. When the judge signed their admittance to the mental hospital they were delivered in a police van. Even women suffering temporary nervous breakdowns were subjected to this disgusting primitive ordeal. Years later a friend of mine became a city alderman. We impressed upon her the need to get this act changed, and eventually she was successful. The law now allows doctors to carry out certification in the privacy of the patient's home.

A smoothly running life has never been one of our family

characteristics, and one day Mother came into my room for a little talk. She had been hemorrhaging for weeks, she told me softly. We were both very dim about the workings of our bodies and didn't easily talk about personal matters. I couldn't offer any idea on the cause, and after a whispered consultation with Harry we decided to take her to the doctor.

After my previous brush both with doctors and hospitals, I was very worried. How did you find a good doctor? The last one had been recommended by a friend, but I wasn't going that route again. Luckily I had an acquaintance who was a nurse. I went to her privately and asked some searching questions about doctors in the hospitals, and how they looked after their patients. Eventually I settled on one whom everyone in the hospital seemed to respect.

Nervously Mother and I went for a consultation. It was a frustrating experience, both for us and for the doctor. How does one talk about bodily malfunctions when too embarrassed to use any descriptive terms? Everything was described in vague analogies, and by the end of the session I was not much wiser about the cause. As for Mother, she was pretending it wasn't her we were all discussing.

The doctor eventually explained to her that when I had entered the world I had "kicked over the traces." I found out later he meant she had a tipped womb. This also explained why she had never become pregnant again. I wish we had found out earlier. It would have saved my many prayers as a child when I pleaded, "Please dear God, send me a brother or sister."

The doctor's verdict was to the point: "An operation is necessary or she will bleed to death." In those days they really gave it to you between the eyeballs. Mother was rushed to the city hospital and I followed as soon as possible. I was doing our old routine of walking to save the streetcar fare when a car pulled up beside me and offered me a ride. Years ago you didn't hesitate to accept a lift from a stranger. This kindly person turned out to be the surgeon who was going to operate on Mother.

He obviously did a good job. When he came to speak to us after the operation, he explained that my mother was the most expensive patient in the hospital. She was the lucky recipient of a revolutionary new treatment. Inserted into her womb was hundreds of dollars' worth of radium, by today's standards a somewhat doubtful honor. To ensure the radium wouldn't get lost, it was attached by a string to the foot of her bed. This seemed a very practical solution, the sort I would have used, and such down-to-earth doctoring restored my faith in the medical profession.

In later years hospitals obviously did not follow this practice. There was a terrible upheaval when an Edmonton hospital lost some radium. It could not be found anywhere and made panic headlines in the papers. Eventually the sewer system was searched at great expense, and the radium was safely recovered.

Mother lived to be ninety-seven, and we always said it was due to her radium tampax.

Thank goodness for Harry's job. There was no health service to help us out, and all this was very expensive treatment. Luckily Harry managed to sell some extra trial transcripts from a complex criminal case. Ours was definitely a case when crime did pay.

7
Moving Up
In The World

Bob and Emily Andison were moving forces in our lives. One night when we were visiting them the conversation turned to the matter of a friend. This enterprising individual had built two houses side by side, one to live in and the other to sell. The problem was that the wife wanted to choose her neighbors carefully and had yet to find anyone she liked.

Harry and I asked careful questions. A down payment was

two hundred dollars, and the full price twenty-five hundred at five per cent interest. The house boasted a living room, dining room, and kitchen downstairs; three bedrooms and a bathroom upstairs; and a full basement. There was even an added bonus. A large workshop on the same lot was rented out to Fane's Auto Body Shop and brought in the princely rent of seven dollars a month.

No wonder I shake my head at today's highly inflated house prices.

We rushed home excitedly and spent the rest of the night sorting out our finances and assessing how many more transcripts Harry could sell. By morning we were ready to make Mrs. Glyde an offer she couldn't refuse.

Hurray! She accepted it.

Though very sad to be leaving our wonderful neighbors the MacOwens, I was tremendously relieved to move off the flats. I'd never vanquished the fear that someday another flood would wash us all away. Besides, we were only moving to the top of the hill, and could stay in close contact with our friends.

Moving day arrived and with it a platoon of Harry's army buddies. Personally I don't know how we would ever have managed without the First World War. Any time we were in a fix, Harry's army buddies turned up to bail us out. It seemed friendships made in the muddy trenches stuck like glue.

The men pitched in. Competently manning a borrowed team and dray, they heaped our possessions one by one. I had misgivings as I eyed the precarious load, but with a cheerful "don't worry missus," the men threw a tarpaulin and leather thongs over the heap, tightened it securely and clicked their teeth at the horses.

The team started off at a spanking pace, and we hoped this would give them enough momentum to tackle the steep gradient of the MacDonald hill. Unfortunately the weather had turned wet, and I recalled a previous occupant of the flats whose wagon not only stuck halfway up, but tipped over — causing all the household effects to roll back down.

Our wagon did make the hill, and I heaved a sigh of relief and returned cheerfully to the concrete castle to organize the next load. I relaxed too soon. The wheels completely bogged down in a mud hole practically opposite our new house. Heaving and pushing had no effect, so Harry had to beg and borrow another team to drag it out.

We were exhausted before the move was completed, and I swore I would never move again. If I had known then how many moves we were to make in our lifetime, I think I would have gone on strike.

Happily settled at the top of the hill, I realized I had left the last of my low spirits on the flats. A new life was ahead of us, and I bustled around cheerfully arranging our few pieces of furniture. This was the first time in months I'd shown any interest in the running of the house, and Mother was only too delighted to sit back and let me create a new home for us all.

Busily involved, I didn't realize Mother was unusually quiet until she suddenly announced she was suffering from a very bad toothache. I couldn't believe it. I'd thought her radium treatment would kill off everything. It evidently didn't stop tooth decay.

With the help of swigs of whiskey swooshed over the afflicted tooth to deaden the pain, Mother managed to bear it for a few days. Eventually we realized it wasn't going to subside, and the search for a dentist became a priority. Literally fed up to the teeth with needing professional help, I found a list and stuck a pin in a name. Wouldn't you know it. The dentist we settled on belonged to the same wholesale school as the doctors.

"They'll all have to come out," he roared cheerfully. With our family it seemed to be all or nothing.

Once again Mother raided her nest-egg, this time with far less enthusiasm. She said she wouldn't have minded so much if the dentist hadn't whistled happily every time he yanked a tooth. Presumably with each yank he was counting the dollars. This had the opposite effect on my mother. For a while, every time she smiled with her mouthful of expensive teeth, I too saw dollar signs — which prompted me to start thinking about a job.

Working women were rare in Edmonton and for a while I kept my own counsel and continued to partake in the social activities in the neighborhood.

Edmonton had adopted the vogue for fashionable afternoon

teas. Being new to the neighborhood I was invited out to several. I hated them.

The conversations were nearly always about babies and I would sit clutching my teacup with a fixed smile on my face. The end came when one socialite turned patronizingly to me and said, "Of course you don't understand. You have no children." That was the last straw. I came home vowing I would start work as soon as possible. My mother could keep the house running and enjoy the neighborhood matrons.

Unfortunately, I did not know what kind of career to follow. The jobs open to women were very limited, and nothing really appealed to me. After scanning the paper several times, I decided to try my luck at an interview at the Rene Le Marchand Mansion. This was a very classy apartment block with one of the few spectacular views in Edmonton, overlooking the beautiful North Saskatchewan valley. This suited me fine. If I was going to work I might as well have an address and a view.

Walking through the elegant entrance hall with its graceful steps and impressive marble fireplace, I felt quite confident and sure of myself. The lady who interviewed me wanted a companion and someone to help her look after her children. She seemed very pleasant, but tired and grey-looking. She confided that her children were driving her to distraction. I was not surprised. I took one look at her battling brats and knew the job was not for me. A good view wasn't everything.

Once again the Andisons brought us good luck. It was at their house I met Harry Hole of the plumbing firm Lockerbie and Hole. Mr. Hole mentioned that his firm was looking for a bookkeeper. I pricked up my ears and told him I'd experience working in a bank in England during the war. He felt sure I would be suitable . . . but? It was a big "but."

His firm shared office space with two other small businesses. One was a tinsmith and the other a paint company. They were all going to share the bookkeeper. I was puzzled. This didn't seem to be beyond my capabilities. Mr. Hole continued to explain that the paint company was owned by Mr. MacFeely who hated the female of the species and English women in particular. He was a strong character and would insist on interviewing me for the job.

Feeling very insecure and pessimistic, I paid my visit to beard the lion in his den. I was convinced I would be turned away. I found the address, a tatty old building with a moth-eaten old Airedale sleeping in a patch of sunshine on the front step.

The dog opened one eye and looked me over. It obviously had no intention of moving. As it was much too big to argue with, I bent down and, very tentatively, patted it. Nothing earth-shattering happened and eventually I coaxed it to move over and let me open the door.

Once inside the office I was very put out to realize I had been under observation. A crusty old character with a tweed cap pushed to the back of his head and glasses perched on the tip of his nose, had been watching the way I handled the dog. This was my first glimpse of MacFeely. The dog was his faithful companion.

MacFeely gazed at me in silence and I felt distinctly uncomfortable. Then, as the silence lengthened, I began to get annoyed.

"Where are you from?" MacFeely shot at me.

I gave him my Edmonton address knowing full well this was not what he meant.

"No, where did you come from before you came to Canada?"

Meekly I replied, "England."

Well! It was like showing a red flag to a bull. He snorted and pulled his cap down over his eyes. By this time I was beginning to get fighting mad, so I stuck my chin in the air and fought back. "And where do you come from?"

MacFeely shoved out his chest. "The United States of America."

I was supposed to be impressed but my mental Union Jack was waving madly, "Oh, and were you born there?"

"I was," said MacFeely.

But I wasn't finished. "And your father, and grandfather?"

By this time MacFeely was looking a little nonplussed, and just kept nodding.

"And how about your ancestors," I continued. "Did they fight in the American War of Independence?"

"I don't know," he growled.

34

I knew I wasn't going to get the job, so I proudly delivered my punch line. "Well, mine did. Not only that, they fought the war on the side of the Americans."

Poor MacFeely. He couldn't have known that my great grandfather's family travelled from America to England in order to find education for their deaf mute child.

So with the strains of God Save the King and The Stars and Stripes Forever ringing in my ears I turned to go.

MacFeely looked at me with a twinkle in his eyes.

"You'll do," he said, "When do you want to start?"

I "did" for them for the next five years.

8
My Guardian Angel

Starting a new job is traumatic for anyone, and I was not the exception to the rule. With shaky knees and a wobbly stomach I slowly walked to work that first morning, wondering if I had made a wise decision. For the first time my life had seemed to be on an even keel; why did I need to swap the local matrons for a man like MacFeely?

The offices of Lockerbie and Hole were on a main road next door to a marble works. As I passed the gravestones on display outside, I hoped that they were not an omen of doom.

Once again I had to coax the dog off the doorstep.

MacFeely was draped over the high counter. He said nothing but gave me a quizzical look. I rather think he'd decided I wouldn't show up. Maybe he was remembering our conversation of the previous day.

The office was very small but attached to two larger buildings. Lockerbie and Hole shared one with Joe Edwards the Tinsmith, and the other was used by Cameron and Company, the painters and decorators owned by MacFeely. It was all very confusing, as I was expected to take messages and do the separate books for all three businesses.

MacFeely jerked his head toward an empty desk behind the counter. I assumed this was to be mine and firmly plonked my bag down beside it and looked around. In the centre of my office was the familiar Quebec heater and behind it a tiny cupboard, which proved to be the toilet and wash basin for all the office personnel. I was appalled; discretion obviously had little place in this office. However, I cheered myself up with the thought that at least it was better than a walk in the cold to the bottom of the garden.

That first afternoon I was left alone in the office, and I panicked. Rushing outside to take great drafts of fresh air into my lungs, I suddenly realized that my days of freedom were over. I missed the open spaces of the homestead and hated that closed-in city feeling.

Coming to myself surrounded by massive tombstones, I looked up astonished to find a serene stone angel gazing down at me. Her wings were folded, and she had tiny white doves and chubby cherubs at her feet. As I gazed at this peaceful marble effigy I decided that she should become my guardian angel. I christened her Alice after a beautiful young cousin of mine who had died at the age of seven.

I returned to the office in a better frame of mind, ready to fill briskly the calls for paint, tinsmithing and plumbing.

The office was run in a fairly relaxed fashion though there were no such things as coffee breaks. We did have an hour off for lunch, and as I lived near enough to scoot home, the walk to and fro gave me some healthy exercise, a breath of air, and a much needed break. I soon began to feel a part of the office and settled into the daily routine.

The free and easy approach between Canadian employers and employees was something I found difficult to adjust to. Accustomed to the old country ways of addressing my superiors as Mr. and Mrs., the relaxed office attitude seemed indecent. Here, no one was ever called Sir. Lockerbie was Doug and Hole was Harry; Mr. Edwards the tinsmith was Joe, Mr. MacFeely was Mac. So it followed that to all and sundry I was Peggy.

Old Mac spent quite a lot of time in the office. He sprawled around chewing tobacco and, when the spirit moved him, expertly spat it into the stove. At first I put up with this dirty habit. I would watch with fascinated horror and wonder if he'd miss. He never did, but one day as a missile shot past me I decided I'd had enough.

"Stop spitting into that stove!"

Mac stared at me with disbelief, his mouth still puckered.

I topped it off. "And you'd better stop swearing too."

He glanced at me with beetling brows and angrily stomped out of the office, slamming the door.

The boys in the workroom later told me that Mac had stormed in shouting and swearing about "That . . . Englishwoman with all her airs and graces." But from that time on he went into the workshop to spit, and his language certainly improved in front of me.

It took much longer, though, to stop his dog using the Quebec heater as a fire hydrant. In fact, I fought a losing battle until the workmen helped me by setting up an electrical shock system. They fixed a wire between the stove and a battery. After a couple of surprises that made his hair stand on end, the dog got the message and found another toilet, outside.

The time passed very quickly, and one day as I was walking past the monument makers I noticed Alice had a wreath on her head. Christmas was coming, and the marble workers had remembered all the trimmings.

Despite the bitter wind I felt warm and comforted by her. "Merry Christmas Alice," I called. "Send us a blessing."

Wrapped in contentment, this year I was ready to celebrate. We now had many friends and several were in the same position as ourselves; few or no relations with whom to share the festive season. We all decided to celebrate by holding a communal Christmas dinner. We hired the Cromdale community hall and decided upon a pot luck menu. We would all take something, turkey and pudding included, and reheat the food at the hall.

The weather had been wonderful. Then Christmas Day dawned and the temperature plummeted, the wind whipped up and a blizzard headed in from the north.

Undaunted, the men set out early Christmas morning and started the fire and got the heaters going. They came back shaking their heads. The hall was such a flimsy affair they didn't think it would ever warm up. How right they were. We packed forty bodies, including babies and dogs, into the hall and turned the heaters and stoves up full blast. It made not one iota of difference; we still needed our coats and toques to survive.

The work involved was terrific. None of us had been used to cooking for such large numbers and we made several miscalculations. But no one was lonely. We were so busy shovelling food in and out of the ovens in an effort to keep it warm that we didn't have time to miss our families back home.

I won't say it was the hottest turkey I have ever eaten, but the company could not have been jollier. After the food shortage in the old country, these frozen but heavily laden tables certainly bore witness to Canada as a land of plenty.

Everyone pitched in to wash and clean up; there were no paper plates to toss away then. Games were organized for the children, and later we had dancing and singing around the Christmas tree. The old magic kept right on working. Sleigh bells rang and Santa arrived on cue to hand out the presents.

This was the signal for a fight to whip up between two small boys. Why do people have the image of small children playing happily together? They never do. The little perishers will fight to the finish over a toy. Disintegration set in with a vengeance when the dogs started fighting. Snarls and growls joined the howls, but at least it distracted the children.

We quickly broke up the party and went outside to find the blizzard had worsened. Who would have thought that snowdrifts three feet deep would have piled up in the few hours we were partying? The dizzying snow was whirling so fast we could hardly see our way to the motley selection of conveyances, and the wind was bitter.

What a mess! Leaving the children and dogs together to keep warm, we ploughed through high snowdrifts in a struggle to reach the cars and horses. Using a few shovels we partially dug out the cars, then used the horses to haul them clear of the drifts.

Finally packing everyone in we drove slowly home.

We made a long and cumbersome convoy, and it took hours as we kept stopping to make sure no one was stuck. The horses fared better than the cars, and in fact hauled several cars out of icy ruts when sheer pushing would not work. Several times the women climbed out to throw their quota of strength against an unyielding rear end.

Everyone decided that the party had been worth the effort, but as Harry and I thankfully climbed into bed that night, and wished ourselves a Merry Christmas, we said "never again."

9
Nipples, Nuts
And Bolts

The telephone rang. "Hello, Lockerbie and Hole," I answered in my best telephone voice.

"Hi. Send me six nipples to the Springer Guest House. Hurry them up and throw in some nuts and bolts."

"Heavens," I thought. "What does he want with six nipples? It doesn't sound decent."

Harry Hole heard me laughing and came in to explain the request. It seems they are part of a special attachment to pipes. He also showed me a lot more queer things that the plumbers might call for.

"We'll make a plumber out of you yet," he said, joining in the general amusement.

Actually, he was right. In the years I stayed with the firm I often splashed around in people's toilet tanks. After all, if you are at someone's house and the bathroom workings don't sound right, it's just common sense to take a look at the ball cock. Most hostesses were unaware that they had a lot to thank me for; unlike the real plumbers, I never sent a bill or told them I had tinkered with their tanks.

Sadly, just before Christmas Mac's dog died. We were all very sorry — the dog seemed to be his best friend — and I felt incredibly guilty and hoped it had nothing to do with the electrical charge the boys had planted on the office heater.

Buster, however, was delighted. Daily he had accompanied me to work, but because I did not want a fight with the old Airedale, I always sent him home when I reached the office door. It didn't take Buster long to discover there was no longer anything to stop him from sneaking in. One day I turned around to find him in the old dog's place by the heater and Mac patting his head. He was accepted into the firm from then on, and often sat under my desk when I worked. Mac never mentioned him, but always patted Buster as he walked past.

Mac continued to amaze me. I was sitting in the office and Mac was at the counter working out some estimates, when a smartly dressed young salesman walked in.

"Hello, is Mr. MacFeely in?"

Mac never looked up from his papers. "No."

Do you know when he'll be back?

"No."

The salesman came back the following day and received an identical response. Once more he tried, only this time he asked for the manager of the paint company. The reply was always the same. "Not in."

Later that day, I saw this young man looking carefully in the windows. When he saw I was on my own, he came in. "Hey, what's with this mysterious manager of the paint company?"

When I explained he had been talking to him all the time, we both had a good laugh. That salesman learned fast. Choosing a good time to ambush Mac, he walked in and went straight into his selling routine. I never found out if he was successful.

Mac lived alone in a downtown rooming house and ate all his meals in restaurants. I've never been a great fan of restaurant meals. Why pay through the nose for something only half as tasty as a meal you can cook yourself? As a Christmas gift, I made Mac a big box of English mince pies. He'd never eaten any before and was quite overcome. He tried very hard not to show his pleasure, but his conversational grunts became decidedly warmer than usual. Though he never did become a talker he continued to show his approval by always asking about my dad. His gruff "Hi, how's Pa?" became his daily greeting.

Loneliness evidently got him down, for just after Boxing Day he turned up at work with a fierce-looking hunting dog. I wondered how that was going to go down with Buster who by now was well established and had favorite warm spots around the office heater, where he could stretch out in luxury even on the coldest winter day. I needn't have worried. Buster was far too smart to become anything but good friends with a dog belonging to Mac.

Harry and I decided New Year's Day 1925 was to be a quiet family time and planned to stay home. After the chaos of the Christmas party a peaceful dinner with Mother and Father seemed very appealing. This, however, was not to be. Little did we know that the city of Edmonton was plotting against us.

In 1923 natural gas had been discovered at Viking, about sixty-five miles outside Edmonton. With great official fanfare it was eventually piped into Edmonton over the Fifth Street Bridge. The gas received a very mixed reaction. Some people rushed out to convert their cook stoves and furnaces while others were more apprehensive, and hung back predicting disaster. We, in our usual fashion, had just not got around to the conversion.

Just as everyone was in the middle of cooking New Year's dinner, the gas pipe outside Edmonton burst. It was a below-zero day, and in no time at all the dinners, diners and houses began to freeze. We had an SOS from two families who knew we weren't reliant on gas, and suddenly instead of our nice quiet family dinner I was faced with a dozen frozen people and three half-cooked turkeys. So much for a quiet New Year.

Being rather superstitious about New Year omens, I wondered what other surprises were in store for us. Sure enough, January proved to be rather disastrous.

Later that month, on a particularly cold night, we were rudely awakened from a peaceful sleep by Buster's frantic barking.

41

Grumbling, I climbed out of bed to see what was upsetting him and saw a glow in the north. I excitedly poked Harry. "There's a big fire in the Norwood district."

"Forget it," said my sleepy mate.

"What me? Forget a fire? Not likely." Flinging on clothes in any order, I was ready for action. Once downstairs I first went to the back door to let in Buster before he woke the whole neighborhood. As I opened the door the rush of night air seemed unseasonably mild, but I just thought the temperature had risen suddenly. Then I realized the glow I had seen was only a reflection in the north. The fire was devouring the Woodland Dairy at the bottom of our garden, just beyond the auto body shop.

Thank goodness Buster had roused us. I patted him on the back and encouraged him to go on barking and raise as many people as possible. I raced upstairs and pushed Harry out of bed. "Forward, march!" I screamed in his ear. I knew his military training would make him react even though lost in the deepest sleep.

It was a dreadful night for those of us whose property was threatened, but particularly for the firefighters. Forty-below temperatures plus a wind chill formed icicles on hoses and noses alike.

Frank McClure opened his grocery shop opposite the dairy and transformed it into instant headquarters. Neighbors took turns brewing life-giving mugs of hot coffee to thaw out frozen firemen and keep them on the job. Everyone in the district was alerted; the flying sparks set fire to several roofs, and many houses were in jeopardy. We all rushed around in the weirdest clothes, making chains of fire buckets.

This disaster brought the whole neighborhood together. Neighbors who had never spoken to one another found themselves working side by side to save homes. We heaved a collective sigh of relief when the wind changed and we were out of danger.

The Woodland Dairy was a charred ruin and took a long time to get back into business. The Edmonton City Dairy apparently helped its recovery. One doesn't often hear of rival companies

42

pulling together, even after that kind of hardship.

They do say things happen in threes, and not long after the dairy fire we had an exciting day at the office. New apprentices were regularly being hired and they were often up to some trouble or other — usually harmless. This time, however, things could have been serious.

Our apprentice was being instructed in the now dead art of "wiping a joint." (Today's joints come ready connected.) "Wiping" was quite an operation. When perfected the result looked like a smooth bandage on a knee joint, the sort any doctor would be proud of. But somewhere along the line the task needed the use of an acetylene torch.

Busy in the office, I was startled to hear a desperate cry from the workshop: "Fire! Fire!" Automatically reaching for the telephone to dial the fire hall, I missed noticing the person who raced past me and broke the fire box on the corner of the street.

I turned around in time to see the men bodily throwing Harry Hole into the street, ripping off his greasy overalls and rolling him on the sidewalk while explaining to the interested spectators, "The dumb kid set the boss on fire."

The men's quick action averted a catastrophe. Harry, though he had to visit the hospital, was not badly burned. His workers also dealt quickly with the small flare-up in the shop, and by the time the fire brigade arrived all was safe.

It transpired that the body rushing out was the unfortunate apprentice, who after breaking the fire box raced off into the distance and was never heard of again. One had to have nerves of steel to work with plumbers.

10
The Great Trans-
Foothills Expedition

Subtle salesmen have always been hard to resist. Our next-door neighbor, Charlie Glyde, was a master in the art of selling cars and no matter how hard I tried to resist him he persisted with the greatest of good humor.

Charlie was a partner in the McLaughlin Motor Company, and it was very difficult to convince him that cars were not one of life's necessities. His pitch was so subtle that one couldn't deal with it; on the surface there was nothing to deal with.

Every week Charlie would drive up with a flourish, in the latest "great buy" from McLaughlin's. The car he would then park outside our house, where we couldn't possibly miss it. Nothing was ever directly said, but Charlie made quite sure the bargain price was dropped in conversation.

For months we put him off, saying we couldn't really afford a car. Then we met our Waterloo. In an unguarded moment, I said *if* we ever bought a car it would be a second-hand one.

That was all the encouragement Charlie needed. Without quite knowing how it happened. Harry and I found ourselves spending the evening going for a drive with Charlie in a very smooth second-hand McLaughlin touring car.

Vanity was our downfall. We really felt snazzy, bowling down the road with the side curtains drawn back and Buster sitting on the wide running board. By now I had been working for a couple of years, and holiday time was coming up. We decided to splurge, and bought the car for $150. After all, with Charlie living next door, and Fane's Auto Body Shop on our lot, how could we go wrong?

Learning to drive was the next step. Driving schools were a thing of the future, so Charlie took it upon himself to be my teacher. Choosing as the safest area a wide traffic-free road called Portage Avenue (now Princess Elizabeth Avenue), Charlie gave me my first lesson.

There were no white lines to worry about, no traffic lights, and the only circles were the ones I made in the dust.

"How am I doing?" I called gaily as I put my foot down, and we sped wildly down the road.

Charlie clutched the side with one hand and his hat with the other. Unclenching his teeth he unsteadily gulped, "Wonderful, just wonderful, Mrs. Holmes. I feel as though I've been on an airplane flight."

Funnily enough, at a later date an ace airman named Willy Post used that same long road as a runway.

It didn't take more than a couple of lessons before Charlie announced I was good enough to go around on my own. Both Harry and I did a little more practising and then offered to take out Mother and Dad.

I don't think we have ever purchased anything that gave so much pleasure to my parents. Mother and Father completely enjoyed those trips in the car. So did Buster. He'd position himself on the running board and balance by leaning on the engine. As always, he saw himself as our bodyguard.

Our confidence grew quickly. There were no traffic police to speak of. One officer had been stationed at the corner of Jasper and 101st Street, but someone took a pot-shot at him one night, though I don't think it was anything to do with his traffic regulations.

After several days of practising around the city, Harry and I decided to take a trip, on our own, to Banff. We felt we needed a break for a while; besides, we dared not risk anyone else's life.

Preparing as though we were embarking on an arctic expedition, we packed everything. At the last minute Harry threw in some mosquito netting. For this we were truly grateful. Except for a few entomologists putting a teaspoonful of coal oil on each lake in Banff, there was no pest control at all.

Mother and Father waved goodbye, and off we roared in high spirits. The first shock was waiting for us not far away in Ellerslie, at what was known as "death corner." Here the road took a sharp turn, just at a point where the railway crossed it. Harry took the corner too fast and we found ourselves in a culvert, but we were lucky. Several people had been killed here, running into the path of a train when they were out of control.

The dirt roads were unbelievably bad. The dust was unbearable if the weather was dry, the roads impassable when wet. Cart wheels had worn great grooves that the car could barely straddle, and once in a set of grooves you couldn't get out. When we safely reached the town of Millet (about sixty miles) we sent postcards home.

We stayed in a primitive auto court in Ponoka the first night, and collapsed wearily into bed so we could be up early the next morning. We'd heard it was possible to drive from Edmonton to Calgary in two days, and wanted to try it.

Sure enough, the second night, tired and travel weary, we triumphantly bowled into Calgary where we slept at the home of our friends, the Knights. Harry was delighted. Cars certainly were an improvement on the covered wagon he had driven from Calgary to Edmonton years before. That expedition had taken him six days.

From Calgary the old carriage trail to Banff meandered around, hugging the mountain sides. I will never forget our first glimpses of these mountains. We were lucky enough to see them on a clear day with a backdrop of blue sky. What a thrill! I gasped at their rugged, soaring beauty.

I gasped for different reasons as the road to Banff degenerated rapidly. The narrow trail had no guard rails. Cars coming in the opposite direction had to scrape the sheer mountain wall to allow the cars on the outside enough room to edge safely past. It was all very hair-raising and dangerous, and we always seemed to be on the outside.

Once safely in Banff we were free to enjoy our long-awaited holiday, staying with yet another set of friends, the Hoggards.

Annie Hoggard was hospitality itself. Not only did she serve endless cups of tea, but she entertained royally. Annie hated stuffy evenings with everyone sitting around being polite. In her heyday she had been a piano player for the silent movies, and she was quite a comedienne.

Each night she seated herself at the piano and entertained us to a running film scenario with appropriate music. As her fingers spun over the keys we heard wild horses stampeding, thunderstorms gathering and lovers meeting. Her soulful rendering of Hearts and Flowers had everyone convulsed.

The Banff Golf Course was already famous and Harry was delighted to play his first game since coming to Canada in such beautiful surroundings. When all the excitement became too much for us we wandered up to the Cave and Basin. This was an outdoor sulphur pool set in the natural rock, fed by hot sulphur springs and considered one of the wonders of the area. We lazily relaxed, up to our chins in water hotter than the average bath. I revelled in it, spending so long immersed that my skin became decidedly prune-like and absorbed the sulphur smell, luckily only for a short period.

Some evenings we dressed in our best clothes and mingled with the guests at the Banff Springs Hotel in order to attend the musical evenings in the ballroom. All this elegance reminded us of forgotten evenings in London, prior to coming to Canada.

Our long journey back was hard to face, so we decided to cut off a big corner by taking a shortcut on an isolated road that went by the Jumping Pound, an Indian buffalo jump. It was in this area, completely off the beaten track, that something broke inside the car.

We were stuck, miles from anywhere, no sign of civilization in sight. Then, right on cue, a farmer with his horse came trotting out of a nearby gate. He soon sized up that we needed help, and he and Harry poked around in the car. The farmer assured us he knew exactly what had broken, but it would take two days to go and fetch the part from Calgary.

My face must have been a study, for he immediately told us not to worry. It seemed he had a blacksmith's shop at his farm and could fix us up with a temporary repair that would get us into town. We hung around the farm for a few hours before we were able to continue our journey, but this was so much better than waiting for two days that I was quite relaxed. After all, it could have been raining.

That thought should never have crossed my mind. Gratefully bidding the helpful farmer a fond farewell, we started on the last leg of the journey, up the Calgary Trail. Unfortunately, it had rained the day before.

Huge mud holes were everywhere. Any travellers were bound to get stuck, so one enterprising farmer had stationed himself and his team by the worst stretch and charged two dollars to haul us through. Actually it was money well invested; most of the rest of the time we spent digging, not driving.

Harry, up to his knees in mud, was frantically shovelling one way when he met a traveller from the other direction doing the same thing. To my amazement they both rested on their shovels, looked at each other and burst out laughing.

Eventually Harry wiped his eyes and said, "I never thought we'd meet again doing the same thing we were doing in the mud of Flanders Fields." The other traveller had fought in the trenches with Harry, and now they were grounded in the mud of the Calgary Trail.

The trip had been marvellous, but we were very relieved to arrive safely home with nothing worse than mud stains and mosquito bites to show for our adventures. A warm welcome from my parents and Buster, followed by hot baths and comfortable beds, made us agree with the old adage, there truly is no place like home.

11
Holmes On The Trail

It was business as usual back at work. Everyone seemed visibly relieved that I was back to take the office reins in my hand. Even MacFeely seemed pleased to see me safely returned. In order to show their appreciation I was given the secret combination number of the office safe.

The safe was built under the counter near my desk. So far, the only people with access to it were Lockerbie, Hole and Mac-Feely. When the need for cash arose, one of them crawled down on his knees beside me and groped surreptitiously with the knob. Occasionally this provoked ribald comments from the customers or anyone else in the office at the time. I think they were very relieved when I had proven my worth. The combination was formally given to me with the comment, "Now you can go grubbing for the money on your own."

Appalled at the slapdash method the men were using to keep track of the petty cash, I firmly announced I would only shoulder this extra responsibility if I could set up a system of bookkeeping that would keep track of the loose cash. The men were quite agreeable as long as it was easy. This suited me fine; I've never been one for a lot of fuss. We agreed that every time someone took money out, he was to leave a note so I could balance the books. All went well until the figures didn't add up. I tackled the men individually, and made them promise not to forget to leave notes.

For a while everything ran smoothly, then small amounts of money were missing again. They all swore they'd left notes. They all patted me on the shoulder and said I'd better brush up my math. This was pretty upsetting. Having worked in a bank I knew I could balance petty cash.

I was convinced someone was helping himself. It was not a daily occurrence, nor was it a lot of money. After keeping an eye on the situation for a couple of weeks I tackled the three men again. They were convinced I was making a mistake.

After several more weeks of growing suspicion, I got mad.

"If you don't do something to find out what's happening, I'm going to quit."

That did it.

One night after the other employees had gone home, the three bosses and I had a secret summit conference. Old Mac's hunting instincts came to the fore. "What we need," he said with a gleam in his eye, "is bait." They solemnly marked some ten dollar bills and with great ceremony placed them at the front of the safe. Sure enough, three days later a couple of the bills had disappeared. I was delighted! Here at last was proof I was not inventing all this.

Imagine Doug Lockerbie's horror a few days later when buying cigarettes from my old friend Sol, he received one of the marked bills in change.

Sol was a friend. We knew he hadn't stolen the money, so decided to take him into our confidence. Doug and I called him in and explained the situation. Sol looked grave. He remembered receiving that particular bill from one of the employees at the marble works next door.

Doug unhappily went to see the owner, Tommy Dikes. He didn't want to cause any trouble, so he asked Tommy to see what he could find out. For a secret operation there were a lot of people getting into the act. We all speculated on the outcome. This was as good as a Sherlock Holmes story.

Tommy came in eventually. At the marble works everyone had been very helpful. One employee remembered getting the marked bill from the corner store. Tommy was obviously as pleased as Punch that there was a simple explanation as far as his men were concerned.

Poor Doug Lockerbie put on his coat and slowly walked up to the corner store. There the trail ended. No one knew which customer had passed it over the counter.

My detective namesake gave me an idea; Holmes had to take on the case for I was convinced it was an inside job. Obviously someone needed to hide in the office and catch the thief red-handed. Doug and MacFeely flatly refused, so I bullied and cajoled Harry Hole into agreeing to hide after closing time.

Harry protested that there was nowhere to hide. I trium-phantly flung open the door of what was grandly known as the stockroom but in actual fact was a cupboard packed with small plumbing supplies. Harry, who was a big man, took one look and blenched. I happily moved a few ends of pipes and made him sit on the floor, then pointed to a spot on the door which, when shut, would just about hit his eyeball. "All we need is a knothole drilled right there and you'll have a perfect view of the safe."

Stifling his chuckles, Doug promised to drill a natural-looking knothole when no one was around.

Reluctantly Harry agreed to try out my plan, and that night we bid him farewell and left him grumbling but safely ensconced in the cupboard.

It seems he waited for a couple of hours and nothing happened. He was very cramped and uncomfortable and just ready to pack the whole thing in when he heard a noise at the office door.

Putting his eyes to the knothole, he was flabbergasted to see a young apprentice walk in whistling as if he owned the place. Pocketing the key and leaving his girl friend on the doorstep, this young man sauntered over to the safe, knelt down and expertly twisted the dials. Harry Hole nearly had apoplexy. The apprentice confidently opened the door and with a flourish extracted two ten-dollar notes.

This should have been Harry's cue to leap out and nab him. Alas, sitting on the floor of a plumbing cupboard for two hours is not conducive to quick action. Harry was stuck. By the time he had unravelled his cramped limbs and found the cupboard latch, the office was empty.

Wearily cursing me under his breath, he tottered over to the street door and opened it to see if the apprentice was still visible down the street, only to tumble over him canoodling with his girl friend in the doorway.

I was relieved to have this episode cleared up, and after this excitement it took a while for the office to settle down to the usual business.

Back at home, Dad was depressed. He worried about being a burden to us. He and mother realized that times were economically tough, for the newspapers continually prophesied doom and gloom. Despite the fact Harry and I assured them two good salaries were coming into our house, they talked things over and decided to find ways of earning extra money.

Mother had what she thought was a brilliant idea. She'd seen an article about a new knitting machine, small enough to use at home and capable of turning out professional-looking garments in no time flat.

Having never attempted to knit, Mother thought this would be a simple and easy way to earn some money. She ordered the machine and it duly arrived to glower at us from the corner of the living room. After confidently embarking on a wool-buying spree she proceeded to cast on. Nothing went right, and as the day progressed she got more and more tangled up in the wool. By suppertime as we cut her free Dad remarked, "Thank God she didn't go in for sheep."

A few days later, this ad appeared in the local paper: "Virtually new knitting machine for sale. Cheap." In all her ninety-seven years, Mother never did manage to knit more than one sock, and a friend did the heel and toe of that.

Dad, although unimpressed by Mother's efforts at cottage industry, decided to try his luck in growing mushrooms. Choosing a dark place under the back steps, he diligently boarded it up and carefully installed a sheet of special glass to let in the selected light rays that mushrooms seem to like. Everything being ready, he ordered the soil, manure and spawn just exactly as the directions said. Then he went into one of his periodic blackouts.

Everything arrived before he came around. The mushroom spawn was not much trouble; it came in a small packet. The soil was a different story. The truck arrived while we were both at the office, so it dumped the lot on the street. Harry and I shovelled and hauled the stuff around to the back steps while Dad blissfully slumbered. The manure was the final straw. That was delivered to the neighbors by mistake, and once again we had to get out the shovels and wheelbarrow.

Dad came to the following morning. Unfortunately he had no memory of his business transactions.

"Mushrooms, what's all this about mushrooms?" he asked. "I'm going to raise a few chickens."

Harry's reply to this is unprintable.

12

Business Dealings

Dad became frustrated and restless. He felt he was a burden on us, and no amount of reassurance could convince him otherwise. Each night, he and Mother would scan the paper, trying to find a small business that they could look after. It needed to be cheap of course, not too taxing on Dad, and something Mother could manage on her own when Dad had his sick spells.

Harry and I were not against the idea but our budget being rather tight during this period, we could not give them too much encouragement.

Scanning the paper each night with the hope that he could become self-supporting again gave Dad a real object in life. He'd see stores listed in the business-for-sale column, mark the address, then follow it up by streetcar. One day he found what seemed to be the perfect thing: a small confectionery shop.

The business seemed to have no drawbacks. Dad looked at the location carefully. It was well situated in Edmonton's growing west end, right by a streetcar stop, and had living quarters attached. Even the price was right, a mere two hundred dollars.

Unfortunately it didn't take Harry long to discover a major drawback. The owner, who had to leave town suddenly, insisted on an immediate cash deal.

What a dilemma. Dad really needed his self-esteem back and we would be delighted to see my parents on their own again. Harry and I had to make a quick decision and we did not have that kind of cash. The middle of the hungry thirties was not the time to be opening a business on borrowed money. Besides, who would give us a loan?

I was sure Harry Hole would help us, but I didn't feel we could ask him. He'd plenty to support with his family of nine children.

The only person who might help was MacFeely. He'd stacks of money and no dependents; maybe he would consider helping us on a temporary basis. I suggested to Harry that he meet with Mac at his hotel that night.

Mac was very relaxed. He'd had a couple of drinks and he liked Harry. I think he was secretly pleased to be asked to help. With a couple more drinks to seal the deal, he promised to join Harry at the bank next day. The following morning Mac backed Harry's bank note and we found ourselves the owners of a business.

The business changed our lives in more ways than one. We soon found out why the previous owner had left town in such a hurry. The health authorities had condemned the store and threatened to take the licence away. The powers that be gave us one week in which to get the whole place cleaned up.

By now it was too late to do anything except roll up our sleeves and spend time and money fixing up the plumbing and cleaning up the mess. No wonder the previous owner had jumped at our offer and vanished over the horizon. We spent the remainder of our hard-earned cash on the decorators — we were too exhausted to finish the job ourselves. The whole experience was quite dreadful.

Finally the dust settled and my parents moved into the apartment behind the store. With a sigh of relief Harry, Buster and I settled down to a quiet life alone.

Permanent quiet was not to be on the agenda, however. Our way of life varied from day to day. We hovered on an uneasy see-saw between a peace not enjoyed in our own house for many years, and frantic visits to the other side of town to keep my parents on an even keel at the shop. Even on the occasional quiet day I was uneasy; I wasn't used to rattling around such a big house on my own with only Buster for company.

Dad showed a lot of wisdom and business sense. He surveyed his stock and realized the key to building up steady customers was to be known for fresh and reliable products. With this in mind he sent for the saleman from the Woodland Dairy and promised to deal exclusively with Woodland if the salesman, in turn, would service the dairy stock daily. He did the same with Boone, the wholesale tobacconists.

This proved to be an excellent move; throughout the fifteen years my parents operated "Lewis's Confectionery" these two men never let them down. In fact they became good friends.

With the store nicely painted business began to pick up, and the streetcar stop outside provided a steady stream of customers. The streetcar drivers soon became good friends with my parents and Dad frequently took rides with them. His favorite route was the journey over the High Level Bridge to Bonnie Doone, the longest streetcar ride in Edmonton. Sometimes he would have a dizzy spell on the journey and the driver would bring him back and see him safely into the shop.

"Sorry Ma, but Pa's not feeling too well today." How kind they were.

When Dad was feeling good, and business was slack, he would take a streetcar transfer and come to see me at the office. One day he walked in just as the phone rang. It was Mother, with a very agitated voice. "Now don't worry. The block's on fire, but I'm all right and people are carrying stock out onto the sidewalks. Don't tell your dad; he'll be too upset."

Of course I had to tell him. He'd heard my half of the conversation. To my surprise he was very calm.

"Is your mother safe?"

"Yes, she is."

He heaved a sigh of relief. "Then that's all right. The fire insurance is fully paid up."

After a disastrous fire in England when our home had burned down, he had always made sure that the insurance was attended to.

Doug Lockerbie bundled us both into his car. We picked up Harry at the police court and dashed over to assess the damage. By the time we arrived the fire had completely gutted the corner store along with a couple of smaller ones, and was just licking the roof of ours.

Eventually the firemen managed to get it under control, and we could breathe again. Mum and Dad came home with us, and we waited for the fire insurance adjuster.

We waited and waited. Eventually an apologetic young man came around. As gently as possible he broke the news. He couldn't give us the insurance because the goods had suffered water and smoke damage only. And because things had been moved out onto the sidewalk, they were not covered. I couldn't believe a system that pays you only if you stand by and let your things burn.

We argued loud and long, and after a lot of negotiations the company gave us a cheque to pay for a massive clean up. The roof was insured by the owner of the building, so we had no problems there.

The cleanup was heartbreaking as well as backbreaking, for it seemed so recently we had done the same thing. The one bright spot was that we managed to have some modern counter fixtures put in along with a couple of booths and tables. Now the customers would be able to sit down and enjoy their ice cream and cold drinks.

The fire turned out to be a blessing in disguise. People were so sorry for the dear old couple who had just taken the store, that business really looked up.

After this episode, Harry and I realized we had no choice but to make another move. It was impossible to keep an eye on my parents when we lived in the east end of the city and their business was in the west end. The fire really scared us. We should be on hand to help in case of another disaster. Changes were happening in our part of the city, anyway. With the boom in cars, Fane's Autobody Shop needed bigger property and was moving out. Now would be a good time to put our property on the market, so we did, and started to look for a house in the west end of Edmonton.

Dad always took a stroll before retiring to bed. One night while walking around a vacant lot he noticed it was for sale. Most people would have walked on — all the lot contained was a small shack with outside plumbing. Dad, however, saw its potential. If we sold our present house we could live in the shack temporarily and build the house of our dreams around us.

MacFeely, who by now felt that he had a real stake in our lives, came over to give us some fatherly advice.

"Before you move, there are some jobs to be done. First, put in some foundations on the new lot and move the old shack onto them. And while in your present home, pull down the building Fane used. There's good lumber in there; use it to build a bathroom and kitchen onto the shack, and you can move in and build the rest of the house at your leisure."

The Glydes were sorry to see us go, but they approved our choice of new tenants. Off we went to start homesteading again, at 125th Street and 108th Avenue, just a couple of blocks away from my parents' store. We sold our McLaughlin and bought a Model-T Ford. We needed an all-weather car. Living in the wilds of the west end meant it was too far for either Harry or me to walk to work.

Challenges have never frightened us, and here was one we really looked forward to. Designing a new house is something many people dream of. Now I had a chance to put into practice my own twopenny's worth of ideas.

Elegance was to be the order of the day. I could see it all in my mind's eye. A large and airy living room with French doors opening out onto the dining room. Of course in my dream all this was accomplished easily and with money no object; in reality there was a lot of unpleasant and very hard work to be done. But the vision kept me going.

As soon as possible, the outdoor biffy was demolished. It's hard to exist on dreams with an outdoor biffy in full view. Once it was removed, I turned my vision to the garden. Now the garden showed real promise. Enclosed by a high fence and with the native bush left on one side, in my imagination it was full of flowers and trees with secluded walks winding their leisurely way through. In reality it was a mess.

For the first few months my dreams of an elegant abode seemed utterly unrealistic. The one thing our lot resembled was a building contractor's yard, an impression reinforced with the arrival of the garage package we'd ordered — fifty dollars, delivered to the lot. Time didn't allow us to tackle everything, so while we did the bulk of the work ourselves, we contracted out some jobs.

Harry and his friends could hardly wait for the walls to ascend so they could tackle the brickwork. One of his army buddies had been a bricklayer; the obvious choice for foreman, he organized our motley crew of helpers very well. It was fun to see people like Bob Andison, the Clerk of the Legislature, handing out bricks to his mates.

MacFeely came up with a handsome gift: solid maple flooring that a client had decided to have ripped out. Mind you, I cursed it a few times. My job was to clean the varnish from the narrow strips before we relaid them.

Design was to be everything, and a steep pitch on the roof was a must as far as I was concerned. It was a struggle to shingle, but when we had finished, it presented the sort of old world charm I had been aiming for. In fact it was greatly admired.

The finishing touches were soon added: a tapestry brick fireplace in the living room surrounded by built-in bookcases; and small old world windows with tiny panes. These were little devils to clean, but again MacFeely had found them second-hand and we were more than happy to make the best of them. Everything was beautiful and I felt myself incredibly lucky. Still despite all these interior wonders, the garden paths were my personal pride.

I'd spotted a great pile of marble pieces at the back of Tommy Dike's marble works. Dropping in to see "Alice" I'd become quite friendly with Tommy. Maybe I could persuade him to help me.

"How much would you charge for a load of that marble?"

He grinned. "Nothing, I want to get rid of it. Just get the boys next door to truck it to your place."

The boys did just that, and in no time at all we had a wide marble path from the front gate to the doorstep, all around the house and down to the garage. There was even enough left over to construct beautiful rock gardens on each side of the back door. The 107th Avenue cemetery had nothing on us. We might not have marble halls, but we did have marble walks.

13
Good Times

We'd started life in our new home with high hopes for the future. I couldn't conceive of wanting anything more. There we were living in the house of our dreams, my parents happily settled in their own business. All I had to do was add the finishing touches.

On advice from so-called helpful friends I called in an interior decorator to help me choose curtains. The poor man was doomed from the moment of his arrival. I knew there would be trouble as soon as I saw him; he was such a fussy little man and obviously had completely different taste from my own. Sure enough he suggested swathes of frilly white voiles and nets. No way! I wasn't going to have my nice new windows all netted up like someone's frilly undies. He departed in a huff and I set out for the fabric sales and the bargain counters.

Poking around sale stalls is one of my delights. I love to find a bargain. Sure enough, the sales did not let me down. There at the back of a stall I found some real fabric; a heavy shot silk in deep orange. Made up, these curtains were a huge success, and neighbors and passersby used to remark on the glow and sheen of the material. In fact when we sold the house fifteen years later, the new owner was so taken with the curtains that she asked me to leave them. I feel sure the frilly ones suggested by the decorator would have been dishrags long ago.

A new house always means extra furniture, and I spent many happy hours haunting antique shops and second-hand dealers looking for bargains. I had a favorite haunt, Reed and Robinson's Antiques, and there I found a very nice Jacobean oak tea table for five dollars. It was a lovely piece of furniture with elegant twisted legs, and I carried it home with pride and stood it in the dining room.

Standing back to admire the effect I suddenly thought, "That's a daft height to pour tea from," so I called in my friendly handyman and asked him to chop off five inches from each leg.

He shuddered. Pointing out that it was a treasure he begged me not to ruin it, but did succumb when I asked him to lend me his saw so I could do it myself.

With five inches removed from the table's undercarriage it made a very fashionable coffee table. In fact, a couple of weeks after the operation a visitor fell in love with it and offered to purchase it for twenty-five dollars. Of course I refused to part with it, and I have it still.

Funnily enough a friend who needed a fireside stool offered to buy the leftover legs from me. I laughingly gave them to her, casting five-inch legs, not bread, upon the waters. Many years later when she was breaking up her home she gave me the stool, thanking me for "lending" it to her for all these years. There was no way could I convince her that the only bit I had given her was the short twisted legs. After much argument I accepted the stool, and fifty years later it still stands and holds my plants, next to the original coffee table.

Everything was going very well in our home when suddenly I smelled a gas leak. It was a very subtle sort of smell and I couldn't quite track down the source. After several days of worrying I called the Northwestern Utilities. Immediately they sent up a man, looking very efficient and bulging with tools.

He tried and tried and could not trace the leak, but he was a very determined young man and not about to be beaten. He tested everything in sight, then suddenly burst out laughing. He'd traced the smell to a cut onion I kept by the side of the sink.

I explained that my grandmother had told me that during outbreaks of the plague, people who kept a cut onion nearby escaped infection. Now that there had been an outbreak of scarlet fever, I remembered the old remedy and thought I would try it. The man said it was the first time he had been sent out to cure a leaky onion.

As he was leaving I had a brain wave. Did he have his pipe cutter with him? He was surprised I knew what a pipe cutter was, till I explained that I was a plumber's mate. Not completely convinced, he asked me what I needed it for.

I took him into the bedroom, and pointing to our old-fashioned metal bed asked him to saw off the headboard. I wanted a low, modern-looking bed to match my new surroundings. He looked at me in alarm, "What on earth will your husband say?" he asked.

"It will be quite all right," I replied airily. "He doesn't have any tools."

So the gas man sawed the top off the head of our bed. He was doubtful that it would stand up, but as usual I was optimistic. I turned the low foot to make the new head and waited triumphantly for Harry to arrive home. When he walked into the room his eyebrows shot up into his hair. They had a habit of doing this, and Harry would pass no further comment.

The bed stayed firm for a couple of months and then one night it deposited Harry and me on the floor. Fortunately my handyman was due to arrive again, so I designed a wooden bar with two short ends for slotting in the metal tubes and holding them steady. This time the bed stood for fifteen years. It would have possibly stood another fifteen, but one night while peacefully sleeping we were struck by lightning. Luckily we were uninjured, but the very next day I traded in the bed for a wooden one.

While we were living a good life, times were changing. We were right in the middle of the hungry thirties and slowly it dawned on me that we were extremely lucky. Not only did Harry have a regular paycheque, but I was also bringing in a steady income. I began to feel guilty, especially when I received a few digs about married women who held down jobs needed by out-of-work males.

It was at this time that Lockerbie and Hole upped my wages to $125 per month. We had a rosy-looking future. I decided to stay two more months at work and bank my huge salary. It was to be my nest egg.

Lockerbie and Hole were horrified when I told them I would be leaving. They felt the organization would collapse without me. I was very flattered but knew this was nonsense and stuck to my guns; the time had come for me to let someone else take over. With a good grace they accepted by resignation and threw a mammoth party to send me on my way. I love parties and my farewell one was terrific. I was deeply touched when they presented me with a beautiful writing desk and a bathroom plunger

— to plunge into my future. The other employees and I had become lifelong friends. Funnily enough, despite our friendship the only times we seem to meet now is at funerals.

In the weeks following my departure, I found that I had a few spare hours. Surprisingly, working both on our house and helping my parents in their store didn't take up the time I had expected. Then I found out that my mother was helping people who were suffering from the effects of the Depression.

The butcher next to the confectionery shop loved the old English dish of tripe and onions, but his family wouldn't touch the stuff; they said they would rather starve than eat cow's stomach. Mother loved this dish and cooked it very well, and once a week she would prepare a massive dinner for the butcher and his tripe-loving cronies.

In return the butcher handed Mother all the bones and odds and ends he would have otherwise thrown out. One of his cronies was the corner grocer, and he contributed wilted vegetables. With these ingredients Mother made great cauldrons of nutritious soup for the derelicts in the area. So I decided to lend a hand in her soup kitchen.

The contrast between our way of life and that of the poor families was painfully sharp. Hopelessly drifting in from the dust bowl of Saskatchewan they looked around Alberta for some kind of work, but nothing was available.

Harry could so easily have settled in Saskatchewan instead of Alberta, and then it would have been us in that desperate situation. I encouraged Mother and also offered to help, like many other people, at the Salvation Army. Edmonton City opened their own soup kitchens, and you could see the long lines of hopeless people waiting patiently in all weathers.

I talked with a mother of five hungry children. She told me the air in Saskatchewan was permanently orange with the flying dust, and that it had filled in the ditches at the sides of the roads. Despite the seriousness of the situation though, some people managed to hold on to their sense of humor. One old wag overhearing us talk leaned over and said, "Aye, there is so much dust in the air that the gophers are burrowing straight up into it to try to get to the sky. You know when the wind drops because it

62

rains gophers."

One day my neighbor, Bea Forbes, noticed chalk marks on the street, from her house to mine. Every time we wiped them, they would reappear like magic. Eventually, we understood their meaning. We lived a couple of blocks from the railway, at a point where the trains slowed down before entering the depot. The out-of-work fellows riding the rods in the hope of finding work elsewhere, dropped off at this point. They had developed a sign language to show other fellows where they could be sure of a handout. Bea and I were obviously marked as soft touches.

The city was not so soft. I was horrified to learn one day that police, mounted on horseback, had ridden into a demonstration of unemployed people who had gathered in the market square, prior to marching on the Legislature to protest the unemployment. I'll never know how those people survived. There was no social welfare in those days. How lucky we are now.

I felt it was time for me to do some regular volunteer work, and there was a call now for canvassers for the Canadian Institute for the Blind. All my life I had been associated with blind people; my grandmother was a sponsor of the Blind Institute in Hull, England.

When the organizers in Edmonton found out that I drove, they asked if I would transport one of the workers, Mrs. Bradly-Saunders, around town. She was the wife of a doctor and a very large and impressive person. When I called for her she swept into my car with her long beaver coat wrapped elegantly around her, and bade me "drive on," as if I were the chauffeur. I would have been very annoyed if I hadn't been struggling to contain my giggles. She looked like a large brown bear trying to fit into a small passenger seat.

In her own way she was quite friendly, and certainly knew exactly where she was going and what she wanted. I quite enjoyed driving her but she did insist on my accompanying her into the various offices. I did not realize at first that she was instructing me in the art of wheedling money out of people, and that I was being groomed to take over her job.

Every visit was basically the same, I would park the car and bundle Bradly-Saunders out, then follow her like a lady-in-waiting. She would sweep into the office and demand to see the director of the firm; no minions for her. When he appeared, and for some reason he always did, we would be ushered into a private office where we would overpower the poor man. Her salesmanship could not have been better if she had majored with honors at the Dale Carnegie Institute.

"How very pleased I am to meet you, and to see that your business is prospering so well."

By this time the victim was looking somewhat stunned; possibly he was on the verge of bankruptcy, but this thought would never enter her mind.

Talking all the time she would gradually lean further and further over the desk until the director was cowering behind it. Somehow she would persuade him to get out his cheque book. That was the fatal move. Once he admitted even to owning a cheque book the battle was over. All that remained was to dictate just how many "doh-lars" the cheque should be made out for.

I often thought the directors made out the cheque in self-defence, just to get rid of us. Sometimes I would see a twinkle in the eye of one of our victims and I would wink back as we sailed out triumphantly like a battleship with a small frigate following. Mission accomplished!

14
Rocky Road
To Vancouver

Nowadays, doctors dispense medicinal dope at the drop of a hat. It wasn't always that way. In my time doctors always asked their female patients how long they had resided in Edmonton. If the answer was seven years or more, they forthwith recommended that the patient spend some time at a lower altitude. We took this advice very seriously.

Upon feeling out of sorts and generally listless for several weeks, I visited my doctor and was given this routine advice. Harry was delighted. He loved a challenge and had been longing for an excuse to visit some friends on the coast. Not knowing what we were letting ourselves in for, we started to plan for what was then a major expedition.

We took our car to the garage for an overhaul, and we borrowed a tent. Using our camping experiences in Banff we then proceeded to load up with the necessary equipment. Our car gave a groan and settled so low on its springs the wheels couldn't turn. We discarded a couple of boxes and threw in the vital maps. We were ready.

The Trans-Canada Highway was still a dream of the future; in fact, there was no road through the Rockies on Canadian soil. We had to be very adventurous and drive down into the States, then up again into Canada and onto Vancouver. I tied my dust veil over my head and we set off in high spirits. After all we had already driven as far as Banff. This trip couldn't have too many surprises for us, could it?

The first part of the trip was exactly what I had expected, smooth apart from the road itself. We negotiated Banff without difficulty and headed out toward Radium Hot Springs, falling in love with it. The brilliant red rock in the spectacular canyon was awe-inspiring. Swimming in the hot springs was a wonderful experience and just what we needed to refresh ourselves. Looking around for lodgings, we found a comfortable little auto court and booked in for the night.

The auto court was owned by a widow who was the sole means of support for her young family. She was kind and made us very comfortable. Obviously needing business, she asked us to try to stay with her again on our return journey. We promised we would. Little did we know that a few days after we left her, a forest fire would sweep through the area and burn her out.

Bright and early the following morning we confidently left Radium behind. I had thought the roads we'd already travelled were the worst there could ever be. I was wrong. Nearing Yahk, in southern British Columbia, was a stretch of road with boulders as big as footballs strewn around and impossible to miss. We bumped and lurched around with our hearts in our mouths. I had visions of being stranded permanently on this dreadful, isolated track. Our bumpers were dented, tires punctured with horrible regularity, and every bone in my body was shaken and bruised.

Years later, travelling a much improved version of this same road, I couldn't help laughing. There beside the road, acting as a safety barrier, was a wall built of rocks which I recognized as the boulders that had been the "surface" of that first dreadful road. Our son Bryan wanted to know how I could possibly recognize them. I said it was because we had hit every one.

Our big moment came at Kingsgate where we crossed the Canadian border into the States. By now we were feeling really adventurous. Not only was this an unexplored road but we were in a foreign country, so off we drove to Bonners Ferry singing "home, home on the range" at the top of our voices.

Bonners Ferry was a disappointment. There was not a ferry to be seen, only a narrow and precarious looking bridge with a formidable warning sign tacked on the side.

"Cross at your own risk," it stated uncompromisingly. Naturally we did. There was no other option. Safely across we thought we would pause and catch our breath over a cup of coffee. We drew up in front of a cafe but never managed to screw up our courage to enter. There on the door was another intriguing sign: "Screen door electrified to kill the flies." It didn't say what would happen to the customers. We backed up at this point and got back into the car. Bonners Ferry obviously didn't encourage tourists.

Driving across Idaho I amused Harry by breaking into song again. Nowadays one always thinks of potatoes in Idaho. All I remembered was a little song learned in my youth.

Little Dolly Day Dreams,
Pride of Idaho.
So now you know,
I've got to go.

This was a tune I'd wound up in my music box as a child, never thinking I'd actually visit Idaho as an adult.

66

Idaho was the first state that made me feel we were in a foreign country. In a very un-Canadian fashion, huge roadside billboards portrayed President Roosevelt and advertised his New Deal and The Five Year Plan. I hoped the plan would include better roads.

Midst all the billboards was one which advertised a place called Moses Lake. It seemed to be some kind of health spa, and after our delightful experiences at Radium we headed in that direction. By now our car was beginning to show signs of wear and Harry wanted to give it an overhaul, so we planned to spend the night there.

Moses Lake wasn't anything like Radium. We drove up to the only motel and were heartened to see it had a sign that said it was a four-star auto court. They could have been sued for misleading advertising. It was a dump, so old, that I felt sure the original Moses must have stayed there.

I was equally horrified when I thought I saw giant turtles sprawled all over the beach. The turtles turned out to be human beings covered in the therapeutic mud. As I gasped with astonishment, one of them spoke. Slowly and carefully, so it wouldn't crack its mud covering, it told us if we stayed three days and bathed in the lake our hair would turn copper-colored. We didn't stay that long to find out, but thankfully bowled out before dawn the next day, relieved to shake Moses' mud off our tires.

Years later, we were again driving through Moses Lake and were astounded to see a most up-to-date and inviting motel. The day was hot and we decided to stop overnight and have the medicinal swim we'd passed up before. Entering the beach in our swimsuits, we were met with screams. I was mystified and found myself watching the water for a landlocked shark. Harry caught on faster and dragged me away. In our absence the place had been turned into a nudist colony. Harry said the name should have been changed to Adam's Lake.

From Moses Lake we'd a long drive to Diamond Lake. This was a shimmering delight. The swimming was idyllic and the whole area remained a favorite spot for many years to come. The lake was especially beautiful at dusk, and here I saw a sunset that has remained with me all my life. The whole sky was a mass of flames, just how I would imagine the Second Coming.

The memory of that sky combined with Emily Carr's paintings are what gave me inspiration to become an artist when I reached my sixties.

While camping around Diamond Lake we met a publicity woman from a hotel in Spokane. She gave us a handful of brochures that spoke in glowing terms of the hotel and described all its amenities, including the wonderful cooling spring showers installed in the courtyards. Hotels always sound like heaven when you're camping, so we were easily talked into letting her make our reservations.

We arrived in Spokane tired out and looking forward to this luxurious hotel we'd heard so much about. The hotel looked as if it had been moved from Dawson City. We found out later this was the intention. The owner was a miner who'd hit pay dirt up in the Klondike, and copying the Klondike style of building he'd hoped to start a fashion and build a hotel empire across the States. I don't think his empire ever got off the ground. The poky hotel room was as hot as hell.

We had been refused a stall in the parking lot because we'd run over a skunk a few miles out of town. That skunk stayed with us the rest of the journey. We had to park the car some blocks away and walk with our luggage to the hotel.

We were exhausted by the time we got to bed but sleep was not to be on the agenda that night. The fire engines next door dashed out frequently; as soon as they returned they roared out again. The lovely spring showers the lady had extolled turned out to be a few sprinklers dripping noisily on to a small metal roof. That also kept our sleep at bay. They sounded to me like cats on a hot tin roof.

Eventually, I stole out in the dead of night with a blanket wrapped around me, found the water tap and turned the damn things off. The following morning the owners were quite puzzled and thought something was wrong with the system. I kept quiet and we left as soon as possible. I wonder how long it took before someone simply tried to turn on the tap.

As the crow flies we were not too far from the sea. All we had to do now was cross the arid desert area between us and Seattle.

68

To modern travellers this area is verdant farmland. It is hard to imagine real desert there, but in the days before irrigation, sand, hot burning dust, blazing sun and shimmering mirages were what weary travellers had to contend with.

We had no knowledge of desert travelling and made the beginner's basic mistake, setting off mid-morning and crossing it in the heat of the day. Believe me, you make that mistake only once.

I thought I was in Egypt and fully expected to see Lawrence of Arabia rushing by on a camel. Sand dunes rolled on endlessly, reminding me of Jack the Giant Killer's residence from the old fairy tales. Tumbleweed bounced aimlessly along the broken fences, and the many dead orchards surrounding uninhabited little homes made my heart ache. I thought of the pioneers who had fought bravely against the relentless drought and given up the unequal struggle. No matter how hot and uncomfortable Harry and I were driving through this area, at least we didn't have to try to farm there. At one little hamlet, a dried up old lady said it hadn't rained there in seven years.

Fortunately, we did have sense enough to take some casks of water with us. Thank goodness. We weren't the only ones who found the heat unbearable. Every few miles the car had a heart attack. Steam would pour out of the engine and we would have to leap out, lift the hood and fan the engine with a blanket to cool it off. Then we'd add a little more of the precious water and try again for another few miles.

What a heavenly relief to drive through the Snoqualmie Pass. It was a cool and beautiful after the heat of the arid desert and we revelled in the ice cold streams and sprawled out in the welcome shade. Even the car seemed to take a deep breath and perk up.

At last we were on the final stretch. We bypassed Seattle and cut across to Everett. Then, Eureka! We saw and smelt the sea. The scenic drive into Vancouver was well worth the week of gruelling travel.

Safely in the Fraser Valley, we threw ourselves into the welcome arms of our friends, the Peacock family. After a night in their comfortable beds we knew it had all been worthwhile. We would face the return trip when the time came. All that was immediately on the agenda was a week in the valley. Just what the doctor had ordered.

15
High Society,
Edmonton Style

Our holiday had given me a taste for the finer things of life. I enjoyed recreation and decided I would carry on with some kind of leisure activity back in Edmonton. Harry, having contracted the golf bug, insisted we join the municipal golf course. The annual subscription was very reasonable, and once we'd joined it cost only a dollar for eighteen holes.

Prior to our visit to Banff we'd had a few games in England during the war, but the only one of any note was a game in which Harry had made a long drive on a Yorkshire golf course and hit a milk cow in the udder. The owner raised hell with him, but the thought of that long drive stayed with Harry. He always hoped to repeat it with a hole in one, and practised constantly.

In later years he was delighted to discover the marble washrooms in the Supreme Court were spacious enough for him to practise his full pivoted swing during lunch hour.

Golf was definitely not my game. I'd be thinking of all the jobs at home and wishing that the slowpokes in front of us would hurry up and get cracking. I was therefore surprised when I was asked to play in a blind competition. In my total ignorance I thought this would be a pushover and willingly agreed.

Imagine my horror when I discovered this meant that the money raised was to go to the Institute for the Blind, not that my partner would be a sightless person. However, I did manage to muddle my way to the final playoff (other players must have been under similar misapprehensions), where I took one look at the city champion and muffed the first two holes. I happily conceded the game to her and enjoyed the rest of the afternoon in a much more relaxed fashion.

That was obviously the end of my golfing career, so to while away the time Harry was on the golf course, I decided to pursue my love of music. Mother had told me about three sisters who were customers of hers. Apparently they sang, so I decided to meet them.

Life was never the same again.

The Crow family were members of a respected English Establishment. Their father had been the Crow of Crow's Liver Pills and I remembered the large signs which peppered the pastoral scenery of the south of England. They were a hilarious family and I was very glad to become friends with them.

Gwynneth, Olive and Essie Crow adopted people at the drop of a hat. They were the warmest folk it has been my pleasure to meet and they welcomed me into their family circle immediately. Gwynneth and Essie were both single and had office jobs, but Olive, the middle girl, was married and home during the day.

Olive became my special friend. All the family were musical but Olive's voice was special. She took singing lessons and practised every morning, accompanying herself on the beautiful grand piano that was the focal point of their living room. She asked me if I would like to join her, so every morning I went over and we vocalized happily for an hour. Olive's work paid off and she often won competitions. My voice didn't quite reach that standard, but I was happy warbling along with her.

You would never believe that the girls were all from the same family, for their faces and builds were quite different. Essie was tall and Olive short and square. Gwynneth was painfully thin even though she could eat out the refrigerator. They shared a musical talent and a great sense of humor, especially about the one man in their lives.

Olive's husband, Joe, was quite small, and the other girls used to joke about it.

"Just look at us," they'd say. "We've only managed one husband among us, and see what a little runt he is."

71

Joe always took this kind of teasing in good part and they were a very happy family.

The girls weren't the only members of the family to love music. Joe was a wonderful pianist, and in his quiet way was the life and soul of any party they held. Not only could he play lovely classical music and accompany Olive in her operatic arias and German lieder, but he was one of those people who could play anything, from the current popular song to ragtime.

One morning, as we met as usual for our musical session, Olive told me she was entering the Alberta Music Festival, so I promised to attend to support her.

At that time, the festival was held in the downtown McDougall Church. It was a very different setup from the Jubilee Auditorium today. The adjudicators were truly British, and usually sarcastic. I think they looked upon the west as a cultural disaster area. I remember one serious competitor who valiantly tackled an aria from Carmen. She was mortified when the adjudicator advised her to purchase a red dress and sing in the middle of Jasper Avenue to get the atmosphere. Another judge, after hearing a quartet, said they reminded him of patient horses working in a cab rank. I didn't want to witness any humiliating remarks about Olive and my heart was in my mouth, but I needn't have worried. As usual she walked off with the first prize.

I was to attend many more of these festivals in my years in Edmonton, but none quite as funny as the year I went to support my godson, Billy Kilford.

That year the festival had been sadly lacking in talent. The adjudicator was a tired individual who had practically gone to sleep during the doleful renderings of the classics. The last competitor was my godson and the prospects for success were dim.

Young Billy was fresh from the homestead and not impressed by festivals. In fact, he was there only under great pressure from his parents. You could see from the way he breezed onto the middle of the platform that he just didn't give a hoot.

Standing very erect, he took one deep breath and at full blast delivered John Peel as if he were on horseback. The adjudicator woke up, quite startled, conferred with his secretary, and my godson, Bill Kilford, walked off with first prize. I was so proud of him, competing as he was against all the city folks and the whole of Alberta.

The other day Bill, now in middle age, took me out in his Cadillac. Passing the old McDougall Church we both simultaneously burst into laughter as we recalled that event.

The musical sessions with Olive Crow fired me with enthusiasm. I decided to dive into my nest-egg, buy a second-hand piano and take lessons from her teacher. Olive thought very highly of this teacher who charged only a dollar a session, and I thought this would be good investment.

The lessons were not quite the anticipated success. I did learn good diction from him, but right from the start I knew he was not the teacher for me. He was very short, and had enormous eyes that seemed to bolt right out of his head.

Poor man. From the very first lesson as he earnestly gazed up at me, I had an urge to plant a pie right in the middle of his face. I knew I would never be able to take him seriously.

He obviously didn't think my voice was a patch on Olive's and so instead of the lovely arias she was learning, I got the Swinging on the Garden Gate songs. I wanted to learn to sing, however, and so I persevered, trying to keep my eyes closed during the lessons.

As well as being an excellent singer Olive was a superb cook, and she orchestrated beautiful dinner parties both for friends and her family. One morning the phone rang and it was Olive with a most peculiar question.

"Peggy, are Canadian sweetbreads different from English ones?"

After I'd controlled my laughter I assured her that the only difference between Canadian cattle and English cattle was the price and the name. In Alberta sweetbreads were sometimes called Prairie oysters, but as far as I knew there were no anatomical changes.

Olive sounded unconvinced and explained she was making a special dinner for Joe, his favorite sweetbread recipe. She'd ordered sweetbreads from the butcher's some days before so he in turn could order them from the packing plant. The butcher's boy had just delivered them, but when she opened the parcel they didn't look right. Somehow they were all shrivelled and peculiar.

The only thing we could think of was that they were processed or dried over here, so Olive decided to boil them first and see if that would improve them.

Later in the day the phone rang again. Boiling had not improved things. In fact it made them look worse, so she had taken them down to the end of the garden and buried them. Joe was going to get something else for supper.

Sometime later that week the butcher phoned Olive and very hesitantly asked how she had got on with the sweetbreads. Olive told him she didn't think too much of the Canadian variety. The butcher stammered in confusion and at last admitted that his boy had delivered the wrong parcel. Instead of sweetbreads Olive had received twelve dollars worth of sausage skins.

By now I had had enough of my pop-eyed music teacher and had decided to quit. While I was wondering how to break this tactfully both to him and Olive, a piano tuner called. Seeing the songs strewn along the top he asked, "Who sings?"

I shyly admitted it was I, but that I had resolved to throw it in.

"Oh, that's too bad" said the tuner. "A new teacher has come to town from Estonia, and she is wonderful. She has a method."

I pricked up my ears. "A method?" Perhaps what I needed was "a method." Besides, it would be much easier to say I had decided to try a different style of music than give the whole thing up. This way I could still practise with Olive.

I got the name and address of the new teacher and promptly enrolled. Little did I know what I was letting myself in for.

16
Hitting The
High Notes

At first sight the so-called studio was not impressive. Tacked on to the back of the bakery and practically nudging the railway tracks, it was hardly the best site for interesting the elite of Edmonton in the complexities of operatic arias; yet this did not deter my teacher, Madame Victoria Nurkse.

Madam Nurkse's husband had died recently, leaving her alone in a new country with only the bakery in which he was a partner as her means of support. This was a very dubious means. More than $600 was owing on the ovens and other equipment, and with the added expense of the funeral Madame found herself almost destitute.

Madame Nurkse, however, had no intention of struggling. She had struggled enough.

Madame had been a musician of some note in Europe. Born in Sweden, she'd become a leading light in the Swedish opera, studied singing in Italy with Galli Curci's maestro, and then sung her way across the continent. Eventually she married a German Estonian and settled down and raised a family in his hometown of Tallin.

Unfortunately they had been caught up in the Russian Revolution and had to flee with their young children, leaving all their wealth behind. Once the toast of Europe, Madame eventually found herself scrubbing floors in the Edmonton Emigration Centre, among other places, to help her husband earn enough money to start the bakery business.

Bereft now both of husband and money she decided to do what she knew best. She, Madame Victoria Nurkse, would teach Edmonton to *sing*. She persuaded the surviving owner of the bakery to allow her to use an empty room at the back and she started to advertise.

While the premises themselves did not look so impressive, the same could not be said of the teacher. There were no popeyes looking up at me here. Madame had presence, with a very capital P.

The rickety door opened to my tentative knock, and Madame towered over me. She was at least 5 foot, 11 inches, with the build of a regal Valkyrie. She gazed at me in silence. Her heavily lidded but piercing eyes seemed to see right through me. Then she smiled kindly. "You wish to sing, no? So ... sing."

I entered the studio and sang for her. She shook her head. "Peggee, you have to throw away all you know and start at your bottom."

It took me several lessons to realize that "my bottom" to Madame really meant my diaphragm.

Madame's method of teaching centred around the diaphragm and was called the Bel Canto Method. Apparently this method had been discovered by very wise old men in Europe. They had watched canaries heaving their little overworked chests in and out, to produce beautiful singing: bel canto.

Madame had several pupils, and we all tried unsuccessfully to act as oversize canaries, but our diaphragms weren't used to that sort of thing. At least we had good music on which to try our trills. Madame had no time for popular songs. She was interested in producing opera stars. You should have heard us trilling our arias, competing with the train bells on the tracks. Bel canto had nothing on us.

I admired Madame tremendously. She was incredibly regal, dignified, beautifully attired, and she worked very hard. No matter what her circumstances she was a lady in every sense of the word. Only her work-worn hands gave any clue to the hardships she had suffered.

The mixture of advertising and word of mouth about her Method soon gave Madame more pupils than she could handle in the back room of the bakery. Much to the relief of all of us (and especially the bakery owner) she moved off the tracks. A better location helped increase her reputation and a lot of young singers came to her. As I look back, I remember such people as Bernard Turgeon, the well-known Canadian opera singer, and Harlan

Green who was lead flutist with the Edmonton Symphony for many years. All were pupils of Madame's.

Many pupils were smitten with Madame's brand of European music, and several of us decided to meet with Madame once a week for an informal evening of music, rather like the old-fashioned soirées. We took it in turns to host the affair in our homes. When it was my turn, Harry helped me move our piano into the entrance hall, open our French doors, and voila! Our home was instantly transformed into a continental salon.

Madame had one very distracting pupil. Miss Willoughby played the cello in the orchestra, but she passionately wanted to sing. Unfortunately her musical talent did not extend to her vocal chords. Madame could not persuade this determined little lady, who wasn't as tall as her cello, that singing was not her forte.

An hour with Miss Willoughby would reduce Madame to tears of frustration. "Why, Oh why, won't she stay with her instrument?" asked Madame, wringing her hands in despair, after a particularly difficult lesson.

Personally, I thought Miss Willoughby was rather clever. She was the only singer I've ever heard who could sing every note off-key. Many people lost a few notes, but Miss Willoughby never hit a single one. She should have been in the Guinness Book of Records.

One night, when the soirée was at our house, this dear soul was delivering Myself When Young in a deep, deep contralto. Several of Madame's younger pupils who were sitting on a long fireside bench burst into uncontrollable fits of giggling. I tried to catch their eyes and eventually managed to persuade them quietly to go and giggle in the kitchen. Stifling their laughter with a series of coughs and snorts, they got up one by one and filed out past her.

Can you imagine! Miss Willoughby was so consumed by finding herself when young, she never heard or saw them leave. At that point the adults had great difficulty controlling themselves as well.

When I hit a high note fair and square, Madame would stop. "Look Peggee! You have made goose pimples on my goose pimples."

One day, I was greeted at a lesson by "Peggee, I have a bone to pick with you. You promised me you would check my gramare. You let me say toppest."

Yes, I had to admit I hadn't checked her as I loved to hear her say "Pegee that is the toppest note I have ever heard you sing."

Madame came to visit me in full force one night, "Now, Peggee. I come to give you a lesson in loff." Love, good heavens. I needn't have been alarmed. It was how to relax my tongue, and produce that beautiful word, "loff."

Madame and I became firm friends, and it was not long before I was invited to call her Vicky. This I did, but when I remember her it is always in her role as Madame.

I never let Vicky down as a friend, but I disappointed her musically. I was not prepared to throw my well-organized way of life away to pursue a singing career. I'd too many other things to do. Madame was disappointed, but as she was all heart she never held it against me.

By now, Madame was a well-known figure in Edmonton. She was not only known for her Method, but was also somewhat notorious throughout the department stores in the city centre. She was always in a hurry, no matter what she was doing, and she had no time for anyone who reacted slowly. Her whirlwind shopping expeditions exhausted everyone but Madame.

Between her lessons, she would dash to a store to buy clothes, allowing only ten minutes. Rushing into a fitting room, with a harassed clerk in close attendance and clutching an armful of clothes grabbed off racks as they whirled past, she would proceed to fling garments on and off at an incredible pace. Her selection was always made at top speed, for Madame never shopped any other way. If the alteration girl was needed, Madame began to fume and look at her watch. The poor salesgirls were overpowered by this imperious lady with her broken English, who was always in such a hurry.

After several years in Edmonton, she decided to take a trip to Geneva to visit her son. Before leaving she asked me to do her a favor. Would I help her arrange a dinner party at the Corona Hotel for her many pupils and friends. Obviously I would, and I asked what it was she particularly wanted me to do. She handed me a list. On it was the name of every salesgirl who had borne the brunt of her frantic shopping expeditions.

I went around to all the stores and invited the girls personally. They were staggered. To date they had only seen Madame the Battle-axe, and now they saw her heart of gold.

The salesgirls were very nervous when they arrived for their sumptuous evening at the Corona. Madame welcomed them effusively, thanked them all graciously, and presented each one of them with a gift. There was only one drawback. After the hearty meal, they had to suffer our musical sobs and sighs, as Madame had prepared a program of operatic arias for their delight. The girls left happy but dazed by the whole experience.

17
An Interesting Condition

I couldn't believe my ears. Here I was, pregnant again! As usual it was a surprise; planned pregnancies had not been invented then — at least as far as I knew. Naturally, after losing three baby girls, I was apprehensive. Wailing "Oh no" at the doctor. I rushed out of his office to cry on the shoulder of my beloved singing teacher. Terribly upset I blurted out my news and told her I would be quitting her lessons. I didn't feel like singing anymore.

Vicky was ecstatic. She clasped me to her bosom with great glee. "My Peggee will have a beautiful baby. She will sing all the time and when she cannot come to Vicky, Vicky will come to her. The new baby will be a great singer."

Well, I was certainly not going to worry about my baby's singing future. I didn't dare think it had any future at all. Perhaps, though Vicky had the right idea. If I threw myself into a round of singing, maybe I could forget that I was expecting. I told no one but Harry, and I was determined to dress to conceal my condition as long as possible.

Nowadays, with young mothers-to-be proudly displaying their bulges with T-shirts proclaiming BABY, it seems hard to relate to the hole-in-the-corner existence we lived when pregnant. This suppression coupled with my utter conviction I would never have a live child made me go to any lengths to conceal my pregnancy. I dieted, wore light corsets and dressed carefully, choosing styles that made me look as though I had put on weight evenly. I adopted shopgirl smocks for working in my parents' confectionery, and made Harry and Vicky promise to tell no one. That way I wouldn't have to deal with commiserations when the baby died.

Harry insisted my mother know — he was frightened I would need her help if I suddenly went into labor — and she too kept the secret. There was no point telling my father, whose attacks were making him increasingly vague and bewildered; none of us expected me to produce a live child.

The exception to this assumption was Vicky. She was convinced that everything was going to be wonderful. She respected my request of silence but made it her business to expose me to lots of music in order to keep my spirits up. "Sing, sing, sing, Peggee" she urged me. "Babies like music." So to keep her happy I continued to warble away, looking more like an overstuffed canary every week.

I gradually withdrew myself from public life though I did continue to drive the car, confident that the steering wheel would conceal any bulges in the months to come.

Despite my early retirement, life became extremely full during those nine months. I met with Vicky several days a week, and running the store took more of my time, for Dad's attacks became increasingly frequent. Mother and I were worried because, as always, he refused to go to hospital.

Eventually the attacks became so bad that our doctor decided Dad needed some emergency treatment at home, but no nurses were available at the time. Before discovering I was pregnant I had spent some hours volunteering with the Victorian Order of Nurses — so guess who was recruited to assist?

80

I was to lure Dad to our house and the doctor would meet us there. He was desperate to try something to bring down Dad's blood pressure. As the rigorous diet didn't seem to be working any more, the doctor prepared to use the prehistoric treatment of bleeding him as a last resort. I was horrified, but funnily enough Dad didn't mind at all.

Dad lay down peacefully on my bed while the doctor and I had a hurried consultation in the kitchen.

"Do you faint at the sight of blood?" he asked.

"I don't know," I said helpfully. "I've never seen any."

He sighed. "Never mind. Get some towels and the biggest bowl you can find and you'll have to be my nurse."

Feeling very professional I gathered the equipment together and followed the doctor to the bedside. I could almost hear my invisible white apron rustle as I held my shoulders rigid and stood proudly by his side in my best VON manner.

The doctor bared Dad's arm. Taking the scalpel he made a slit just above the inside of the wrist.

Up shot the blood like a Yellowstone Park geyser. It hit our bedroom ceiling and made a horrible mess. I let out a yell and the doctor gasped.

"My God, I never expected that. Why the devil won't the silly old man go to the hospital?"

He managed to channel the mad flow of blood into the bowl. Within minutes it was full, and he passed it to me to take out to the toilet. I passed out.

When I came to, Dad was lying peacefully asleep in bed, I was propped up in a chair, and the doctor was down on his hands and knees with a bucket, cleaning up the mess.

We were very lucky with that doctor. He never grumbled about my so-called assistance and he always came quickly to attend to Dad, whether it was a day or night call. When it became necessary to bleed Dad it was never quite so bad as the first time.

Ignoring my pregnancy seemed to work. I sang regularly with Vicky and felt better for it. In fact I was feeling so good that one day I had a brilliant idea. Mother's birthday was to be on June 21, the longest day of the year. Why not hold a big garden party for her? I felt confident that no one could guess my secret as I

81

looked just a little plumper.

I rushed home and invited our large circle of friends, and also extravagantly phoned England to invite Mother's sister as a special birthday surprise. To my delight she promised to come, and booked her trip out immediately. The two sisters had not seen each other for more than ten years.

Little did I realize what a tradition I had started that day. The Birthday Garden Party was so successful that it was repeated every year until Mother's death at the grand old age of ninety-seven.

I will never forget that first party. Our garden was beautiful. All the plants were well established and in full bloom. For the first time I realized how far we had come in our years in the West. No longer were we struggling to scrape a living from a ground that was reluctant to yield. We had a beautiful house and a verdant garden that looked as though it belonged in the pages of a glossy magazine. As the guests walked up the marble pathways they were duly impressed. It was a perfect party.

Mother and her sister were delighted to see each other again and we had a very happy time showing Aunt Nelly the sights of the West. In her true English fashion she kept a stiff upper lip, though admitting to being "quite impressed with Canada," particularly when we managed to fit in a trip to the mountains.

Aunt Nelly was completely overawed by Banff. With a brilliant blue sky as a backdrop, the Rockies showed her their best side — just like in the photos on boxes of chocolates. She was almost speechless and obviously felt overpowered and even claustrophobic in the valleys. We heard that when she got back to England, however, she said nothing of the mountains but held forth to the Women's Institute about "the evergreens of Canada." I would have loved to have heard that speech.

By now I'd almost forgotten I was pregnant. The game of concealment had become second nature, and looking after my parents kept me busy. My friends had obviously noticed that I wasn't available any more, but we blamed it on Dad's deteriorating condition and they seemed to accept our explanations. On the very few days I felt off-color and unable to attend my singing lessons, Vicky gave me no choice. She would arrive at my door with a wide smile and armful of flowers. How could I refuse?

The weeks went by and we still kept my secret. In fact I could hardly believe it myself, I felt so well. The summer of 1935 was so beautiful that Harry managed to persuade me to go with him for a quiet week at Waterton Lakes. It was very peaceful there, having not yet been discovered by the tourists. I felt confident that no one I knew would see me, and puttered gently around the golf course in Harry's wake.

Summer turned into the fall and as the days grew shorter the time of the birth approached. Eventually I had to visit a gynecologist, but I wouldn't pin my hopes on his cheerful assurances that all was well. I had heard those tales before.

One chilly November night Vicky had dined with us, and we had sung lustily till it was time for Harry to take her home. I had been plagued with a backache all that day but the singing had taken my mind off the discomfort. Suddenly, after Harry had left, I realized the backache was attacking at regular intervals. I was terrified. Never had that house seemed so big or so empty. I sat in the hallway and cried.

Buster came running and sat beside me while I clutched him to me and hid my face in his fur. How was I going to get through the next few hours' agony? He licked my face, whined and placed a comforting paw on my knee. Somehow I found the courage to drag myself to the bedroom and throw some things in a suitcase. By the time Harry returned I was sitting with my bag packed. We drove immediately to the University Hospital.

A nurse cheerfully received me in the new maternity building and assured me that they hadn't lost a baby yet. This was music to my ears and I tried to hang on to her words throughout my prolonged and exhausting labour. By now I was in my mid-thirties and my body protested vigorously at the strain I was putting on it. It seemed a long cruel struggle when I was convinced that the outcome would be more unhappiness.

This time the specialist was on hand. Not only was he a good doctor, he also took me in charge mentally. "Let's have no more talk about dead babies," he ordered. "I'm a Rosicrucian and I have a whole church group praying for you."

Well! I couldn't let down a group of good people like that. I did my best to cope and thirty-six exhausting hours later, just ten years to the day of the birth and death of our twin daughters, I delivered a fine healthy baby boy, Bryan Lewis Holmes.

Harry was ecstatic, and after all these years everyone else expected me to be the same. Unfortunately I was terrified of the child. Years of not daring to think about a live baby had left deep scars. I found I was unprepared to cope. I had buried all the normal anticipation and made no preparations at home for the new baby. I didn't even know how to bath or diaper him.

Luckily, after the shock of finding out her daughter had finally managed to produce a bouncing grandchild, my mother came to the rescue. She had the necessary equipment ready for us when we came home from the hospital.

Young people today don't realize how much of the dark ages we lived in. Prenatal care, maternity classes and postnatal care were things I had never heard of. The only information I was given upon leaving the hospital was, "Keep the bathroom warm."

This I took literally. Terrified of little Bryan catching pneumonia, I turned the furnace up so high I nearly passed out. Harry took one look at my first struggles to handle the child and he called in the VON to help. Thank goodness. They saved young Bryan from some very trying experiences and taught Harry and me basic child care. Harry was the perfect father, and in fact when Bryan was put on the bottle it was Harry who got up to give him the midnight feeds.

Suddenly Harry gave up smoking. I was very puzzled; he had been a heavy smoker for years. Finally it came out that one night while giving Bryan his feed he'd accidentally dropped an ash on his son. This scared him so much that he had instantly stopped smoking.

We soon got into a routine, though I did wonder how faithful old Buster was going to take the new development. I settled down beside him and fondled his ears while telling him all about the new baby. I introduced them and told Buster he would have to guard Bryan. This dog who had been used to rounding up cattle and fighting with coyotes understood every word I said. He was Bryan's faithful bodyguard and wouldn't let any strangers touch the baby buggy now that he'd been told to look after it.

Vicky of course took full credit for the whole business. She was convinced that the music had relaxed me and allowed the baby to develop into a strong healthy boy. She could have been right about that but she was wrong about him being a singer. To this day Bryan doesn't sing a note.

The only real problem was my father. Because I had kept my pregnancy secret, he never did believe Bryan was our child. He was very happy with the new baby and would walk proudly around the block pushing the buggy. "Yes," he would tell the admiring passersby, "this is my new grandson. They adopted him."

18
Being "Done" Right

Routine and organization were gone. So was the quiet life, but it was wonderful to have a baby in our small family. Once I actually got used to handling Bryan and realizing that his arms and legs didn't drop off, my only fear was that he would be spoiled by too much attention. Because he was such a surprise to everyone, all our friends made a great fuss of him and the presents and good wishes came pouring in.

Sometime after his birth the rumors circulating the district came to my ears. I was flabbergasted when I realized Dad still thought Bryan was adopted. Nothing we could say made any difference to him; it just didn't sink in. Oh well, as long as he loved the child I could cope.

Harry had always been a thinker, and in his own quiet way was always searching for the true meaning of life. At this period he was delving deeply into the mysteries of the Rosicrucian philosophy. In fact, he was currently the Master of the Lodge. He had tried to encourage me to look into their teaching and I read some of their lectures, but I decided it was far too deep for me. Harry never seemed to mind me not going with him to the lodge but one day broached the subject of Bryan's christening. How did I feel about a Rosicrucian christening?

I thought it over. It seemed a reasonable request and after my experience with the doctor who had his fellow Rosicrucians praying for me, why not? I had met some members of the local church and they were pleasant people. It would probably raise a few eyebrows in the neighborhood, but I had been doing that all my life. We settled on a date and I looked forward with interest to the ceremony.

The Rosicrucian lodge was above Read and Robinson's store, the second-hand shop where I'd found so many bargains. The meeting room was primitive, though above the platform where they conducted their ceremonies the enthusiastic members had painted a desert scene with a pyramid and a somewhat coy camel. It looked impressive.

The christening was a very happy and reverent service and certainly spectacular. Our baby was laid before the pyramid in order to benefit fully from its power and wisdom. Then the devout acolytes, lovely young girls who swayed around Bryan, swung incense and sprinkled rose petals over him. The singing was absolutely beautiful, and the atmosphere was joyous.

After the ceremony we adjourned to our garden for a party and celebrated in a more secular way. There I learned that Bryan had made history. He was the first baby to have been christened in the Edmonton Rosicrucian Temple, and everyone was very proud of him.

Later that week I kept going over to Bryan and looking at him. He seemed perfectly happy and contented, but something kept niggling at me.

What if he hadn't been "done" right?

Suppose rose petals didn't count?

A very good friend of mine, Flora de Wynter, was arranging a christening for her baby, Joan. I went to visit her and told her of my secret worries. We talked things over and Flora in her down-to-earth way said, "No sense worrying about it. Do him again with our Joan."

I told Harry that I wasn't convinced rose petals worked but that a double christening in the Anglican Church of St. Stephen might do the trick. Harry had no objections, and this time 'round the de Wynters stood as Bryan's godparents. With the strains of Fight the Good Fight ringing in our ears, I felt our child could truly own his name, Bryan Lewis Holmes.

Once again we celebrated with a sumptuous garden party. What with all the good wishes, rose petals and holy water, not to mention the wonderful food, young Bryan should have a rosy future ahead of him.

As a child in my Yorkshire home in England, I'd always been told, "Never turn a stranger away from the door; it might be Jesus." This command was carried out with persistent regularity in both my parents' and my grandparents' homes. A nourishing soup was kept in the pantry, ready for the pot. My family never intended to be caught napping at the Second Coming, and now in western Canada I tried to continue this tradition. It never occurred to me that a woman alone with a small boy might be vulnerable.

One twenty-below-zero night I was cosily preparing a meal for Harry. He was due home from court any minute, and I had arranged for us to have a quiet dinner together. Bryan was fed, contented, and almost asleep, and a quiet peace prevailed.

Suddenly there was a loud knock at the kitchen door. It startled me and I dropped the soup ladle. Upon opening the door I saw a young man. Fair haired and tall, he was painfully thin and not dressed for the bitterly cold weather. His old coat was threadbare and he had no cap or gloves. He was almost blue with cold.

"Come in and get warm," I begged. "You must be freezing. Besides, I must close the door or the baby will get chilled."

Bryan gurgled his delight at this unexpected visitor, and the young man looked longingly at him. To my dismay I noticed two large tears rolling down the fellow's cheeks. Brushing them away, he told me he had left his young wife and baby son back east while he came west looking for work. Seeing us well fed and warm was almost more than he could bear.

My heart was deeply touched and I sat the tearful young man down to a good meal and gave him some money. Wishing him luck I sent him on his way and he thanked me profusely, and gave us his blessing.

Harry arrived home soon after the stranger had left. Naturally I was full of the visit, and graphically related it in detail and with all its pathos.

Concerned, Harry was not at all happy that I had let this stranger in. He felt sure he had been riding the rods and was a bum. He tried to make me promise only to give food and money, and not invite strangers into our house. The joy disappeared from our evening and I was upset. This had not been our code back home.

Arriving home the following evening, Harry again asked me to describe "the bum" as he called him. I did so in detail, all the time wondering why he wanted to drag up the now unpleasant incident.

"Did he tell you his name?"

"Of course," I answered. "He was very well mannered. He was called Paul Wilson."

"Well!" said Harry "Let met tell you that when court resumed at two this afternoon, I read your Paul Wilson the charge of robbery-with-violence."

This same young man, with a gun in his hand had robbed and threatened a blind man, Scotty Files, who ran a small news store on Jasper Avenue. Paul Wilson had pleaded guilty to the charges and would receive many more free meals before he found work in the West.

Did I learn a lesson? No. I'd do it again. The thought of Paul haunted my dreams for many weeks. Who knows what desperate straits he was pushed to. Besides, the next strange caller at our house might be Jesus.

Bryan progressed by leaps and bounds and it was a great joy for me to push my baby in his carriage around the district, with Buster at our heels. Of course, we always popped in to Lewis's confectionary to visit the grandparents, and most of the customers stopped to visit with Bryan.

Being around adults who talked constantly, Bryan spoke at a

very early age. He was less than a year when upon our return from a trip to the coast we dropped into the store to visit with my parents. Seeing Bryan sitting upright in his baby carriage, a customer playfully tickled him and asked "And where have you been, young man?" To his amazement, Bryan in a clear voice replied, "Bamcouber."

I don't know who looked more startled, we or the customer.

Bryan was a strong healthy child. Of course, like all parents, we had our ups and downs. When he was as high as the kitchen counter he ran into the corner and hurt his head. I dashed for the saw and hacked the corner off.

It was a rough job of carpentering, and I laughed when fifty years later I went to visit in that house and noticed the corner was still sliced off. Someone had smoothed and rounded it though, and it looked better than when I'd done it. Back then I little thought Bryan would be six feet tall.

I had always encouraged Bryan to be independent and I have never regretted that decision, though there were drawbacks. He chose his own friends and sometimes they taught him unacceptable words. At one Christmas party some adults were playing a table game, something like a mini-shuffleboard. My curly-headed small child, encouraging them to win, shouted, "Shove it up the bloody alley!" You can imagine the shocked silence from the adults and the meaningful glances exchanged over his head.

Luckily, at this period Margaret Ingram popped into our lives. Margaret had come from England as an exchange school-teacher. After a whirlwind romance she became Mrs. Tom Ingram and that was the end of any idea of returning to the old country. She arrived for tea one afternoon in a quite agitated state. Some of Bryan's little pals had shouted obscene words as she entered our gate. She collapsed in a chair and wanted to know if those were Bryan's playmates. I had to admit they were.

Margaret regained her composure and made a suggestion. "Peggy, this won't do. Bryan is becoming a young ruffian. Now, if you can get ten other mothers with small children I will open a kindergarten. I was trained in the Montessori Method. Bryan and his friends can be my first pupils."

This appealed to me and I felt sure I could gather ten pupils, but where would we hold the school? Our house wasn't big enough.

Tom, Margaret's husband, was a well-known contractor around town, but the Depression had caused business to slacken and he had a little time on his hands. He was quite happy to turn the top storey of their large home on 124th Street into a school, and offered to make the desks and small furniture — and to help in every other way possible.

So Lynwood School became a reality, and all it needed was for me to drum up the pupils. We not only drummed up ten, but had reached twenty when Margaret said, "Stop! I can't handle any more."

What a blessing this kindergarten was to the mothers of the district. The children not only learned the Montessori Method — whatever that was — but they learned good behavior. Bryan's manners became so fine that sometimes they landed him in trouble.

A lady came knocking at my door one afternoon.

"Come to the corner. Your young son is up to his waist in mud and refuses to let anyone help him."

There had been a drowning in a mud hole a few days before, and I madly dashed to the corner. Sure enough, there was Bryan, waist deep.

I dragged him out, asking, "Why didn't you let the lady help you?"

"I hadn't been introduced," replied my son.

19
Nine Days

Some years are a penance to live through. For me, 1937 brings back memories I would much rather forget. My father, after struggling with chronic illness for years, was now constantly ill. The sudden lapses of memory and the blackouts he suffered became more regular. But what was even more difficult to deal with was his change in personality. No longer a quiet but fun-loving man game to try most things, even the wild west, he began to have queer delusions about the people around him.

Dad spent very little time in the store, so the burden of keeping it open fell to my mother. I did my best to look after Dad, but sometimes the situation was very hard to deal with.

One day I tried to stimulate my father's mind. He was having a "silent period" during which no one seemed able to get through to him. Thinking that a change of scene might help, I took him for a drive along the river. The day was beautiful and the sunshine sparkled on the water. We drove slowly along, stopping to watch the tiny waders at the water's edge and even a determined little muskrat who was trying to beat the current and swim across to the far side.

Suddenly Dad turned to me. "Now I know what you want me to do," he said slowly.

"What do you mean?" I asked.

"Well," he said, "you want me to go in that river, don't you?"

The impact of having a parent say something like that is incredible and I really didn't know how to deal with the situation. To this day I don't know how I managed to get us safely home. All I can remember is how horribly upset and helpless I felt.

As always Harry was practical. "While he's got things like that in his mind," he said, "you'd better not take him by the river."

That was the best we could do. Mental illness is difficult to deal with now, and all those years ago it was well-nigh impossible unless you were so desperate that you certified the patient.

Summer was in full bloom, and Harry and I were due to go away for what had become our annual holiday at the coast. As usual we left a friend, this time Bob Andison, to keep an eye on my parents. That way we could relax, knowing everything would be all right while we were away.

My mother and father came to say goodbye to us outside the little store. I can still see them in my mind's eye. They stood waving happily as I turned 'round to look at them before our car took the corner. I was very quiet as we drove out of Edmonton, and when Harry asked if anything was the matter, I said I had an awful feeling that I would never see my father again.

We drove to Calgary without incident and I was very relieved to see the lights in the distance. There we were to pick up a friend, Leola Knight, who would accompany us to the coast. After trying desperately to keep young Bryan occupied between Edmonton and Calgary, I looked forward to someone who could spell me off during the long journey through the mountains.

As usual the coast was beautiful and well worth the difficulties of the journey out. This time the long trip had actually gone faster. Bryan kept us on our toes. Anyone who has tried to entertain an active little boy confined to a car for several days will know exactly what I mean.

Bryan was ecstatic when he saw the sea, and delighted when we promised him that after a short visit with the Peacock family in the Fraser Valley, we would go to White Rock where we had booked into an auto court right on the beach.

We had a very pleasant visit with George and Phyllis Peacock in their lovely Fraser Valley home, but Bryan was desperate to play on the beach and paddle in the sea. Off we went to White Rock, with George and Harry promising to meet later that week for a fishing trip. George would phone the local store at White Rock and leave a message telling Harry when he could get a free afternoon.

The auto court and the weather were all we expected, and Bryan and I had a relaxing time exploring the beach and sun-bathing while Harry pottered around talking to the local fisher-men. Eventually the storekeeper said there was a message for

Mr. Holmes, and Harry went off happily to arrange his fishing trip.

He had a most peculiar look on his face when he arrived back at the auto court. It was George who had phoned, but not about the fishing trip. Bob Andison had been trying to get hold of us.

"There's a little trouble in Edmonton," said Harry, "but try not to worry. Your father is missing. "Missing," I said. "Missing?"

I immediately started to pack while Harry went to find out the best way to get to Edmonton in a hurry. Never before or since have I felt Edmonton was quite so isolated as I did then.

We decided Bryan and I would catch the train to Vancouver, then change for Edmonton. This way I could be with Mother as fast as possible. A train was waiting in the little station at White Rock. I threw as many things as I could in a suitcase, grabbed Bryan off the beach, and Harry bundled us on with three minutes to spare. Harry and Leola would have to drive back later.

The train journey was unbearably slow. I had never noticed before how many bridges and rivers the line crossed, but on this journey I was aware of every one. In my wrought-up state every glimpse of water told me my father had drowned.

Arriving in Edmonton I found the whole town was in an uproar. The police were out searching, there were calls on the radio, boy scouts were beating the bushes, everyone was upset and doing the utmost to help. There were no clues about what might have happened and I hated to see the newspapers each night, with their headlines: Elderly Man Still Missing.

Eventually my father's hat was found some blocks south of our house, in the general direction of the river. I could not get those strange comments of my father out of my mind, even though they had been spoken months before. But because we lived so far from the river, no one in Edmonton thought drowning was a possibility.

Meanwhile, Harry was driving back as fast as he could. He phoned from Calgary to say that Leola had very kindly arranged her family affairs so she could come straight up to Edmonton to help us. A day and a half later they arrived, much to my relief.

It was on the ninth day when we had a call from the Mounted Police down the river, about ninety miles away. An unidentified body was about to be buried out there; would Mr. Holmes like to come and check it out?

We have been involved in many strange situations but this coincidence was the oddest. An Edmonton commercial traveller used to come to our store and knew my mother and father very well. Like most people in Edmonton at this time he knew my father was missing.

He was visiting one of his customers in the small community of Wasa, ninety miles away, and they were chatting over a cup of tea.

"We will have a sad burial here today," said the storekeeper, "an unknown man. His poor family will never know what has happened to him."

The traveller asked what had happened and the storekeeper explained that a man's body had been washed up on the river bank not very far away. The local police hadn't any idea who he was, and they were burying him that afternoon as an "unknown body."

The traveller was quick on the uptake. "Mr. Lewis is missing," he thought. "Could this be him?" So off he went to the local police and asked them to delay the funeral. The Wasa police got in touch with Edmonton, and then with Harry.

It seemed very likely it was my father, but the body was in a bad state and a positive identification would be difficult. All they knew for certain was that it was an elderly male.

Harry immediately drove out to identify the body. It was horribly battered and quite beyond recognition. Then he noticed the boots. Battered and water-damaged they were, but unmistakably my father's boots.

It was a dreadful ordeal for Harry, but the end of the waiting for us. The Edmonton police were very angry that the police in Wasa hadn't notified them about the body and there was some talk of the constable concerned being cashiered for neglect of duty, but we wouldn't press charges. Nothing could bring my father back, and despite the constable's negligence a strange coincidence meant he wasn't buried in an unmarked pauper's grave. We were relieved to have the uncertainty over and there was no earthly good making someone else suffer.

Gradually we managed to piece together my father's last day. On that evening some friends offered to take him for a drive. Mother was pleased as he liked to go out whenever he could. These people took him for a drive by the river. Eventually they brought him back to the shop, but noticed that he didn't go straight in. They knew he liked to stretch his legs after sitting for a while, so thinking he might take a walk they waved goodbye and drove away.

Later a customer met Dad on 124th Street and said "Good evening." Dad said "Good evening," but didn't reply when the customer asked if he was going for a walk. The customer thought this odd, but maybe Dad hadn't heard. Dad carried on walking south.

And that was the last anyone saw of him.

The doctor tried to comfort us all. He explained that fifteen years of blackouts could have damaged Dad's mind and caused destructive delusions. Even more simple was the explanation that he could have been going for a quite innocent walk, passed out and lost his footing.

We will never know. Either way, he was gone and we missed him.

For many years after that, the rapidly running river water seemed to want to suck me down if ever I went near it. I could always visualize my father and it was a long time before I could face a stroll on the river bank.

Then my common sense reasserted itself. How ridiculous. Other people have died in hospitals after lingering illnesses; to them Dad's sudden death would have seemed a merciful one.

20
England, Their England

Tragedy always changes one's life. The shock and strain of Father's death aged Mother. She lost her voice and her hearing was impaired, both a reaction to the stress. The doctor had no way of knowing if these faculties would ever be restored, and he ordered a complete rest for her.

My nerves were raw as well and I suffered from horrible flashbacks of several worrying scenes with my father. Particularly haunting was the memory of that drive by the river, and my father's terrifying comments. I kept wondering if I could have handled the situation any differently, and if the outcome would have been the same.

Mother was unable to look after the store, and I was weepy and even more unpredictable than usual. Obviously a change of scene was needed in our family.

After a family conference. Harry, who had no more leave at that time, came up with a plan. We needed a competent worker in the store anyway, so why not get full-time help instead of part-time? With the store out of my hands, Bryan and I could go off to England and Mother could rest. She and Harry would follow us over when his vacation came through.

This was a tempting offer. It was nearly twenty years since I'd come to Canada. We'd family and friends in England, and they'd extended warm invitations many times. A trip to my homeland sounded very good, and the idea re-activated my curiosity in life. Besides, it would be interesting to introduce three-and-a-half-year old Bryan to his relatives.

My nervous condition made it hard for me to come to a fixed decision, so Harry rushed out before I could change my mind and booked us passage on the Cunard liner, the Asconia. Everyone assured me that children were always good travellers and I would have nothing to do on the journey except lie back and enjoy the bracing salt air and the good food.

So much for good intentions. The train journey to Montreal was tedious and horrible. I'd too much time to think during the day and could not sleep at night for bad dreams. Was this what the doctors ordered as a complete rest? After carrying an intolerable burden of responsibility for so long, I found I could not put it down. It was impossible for me to rest.

Luckily I had Bryan. Without him I think I would have been insane by the time the train reached Montreal. Bryan was into everything. Just as I would be wallowing in self-pity he would vanish and I would have to go searching up the train for him. He made friends with the conductors and passengers in every carriage, kept me aware of mealtimes and generally provoked me out of depressive fits.

By the time we reached the dock I was looking forward to the restful voyage everyone had told me about. The air had a nice salty tang, and the gulls cried and wheeled above us.

We carefully boarded the Asconia, Bryan dancing and hopping around excitedly. As I fumbled with our tickets and boarding pass I realized that all the other people seemed to know what they were doing and where they were going. I'd always had Harry with me and now I was going to have to think for myself. In my unstable state I did wonder how all this change could really be the answer to my problems.

The first thing I was aware of on the ship was someone shouting, "Who does this kid belong to?" Horrors! There was Bryan's backside and legs — the rest of him was hanging through an open porthole. I didn't dare call to him in case he lost his balance, so I crept up and grabbed him by the seat of the pants. From then on I didn't have a minute's peace. A small child in a large liner is a menace. I was terrified that he would fall through the open spaces beneath the lifeboats.

As for the advice I had been given about travelling with children? I threw that out the porthole on day one. My poor little terror was ghastly seasick.

At our first sitting for dinner, I listened with interest to all the accents around us. It was very exotic.

"I wonder what nationality our waiter is?" I remarked to a fellow traveller. "I can't understand a word he says." Laughingly he replied, "You should be able to understand him. He's a cockney."

This was my first inkling that returning to England was not going to be as simple as I'd imagined. Twenty years is a long time.

Arriving in England I could not understand why I felt worse than when I left home. Everything seemed almost the same. The people were all a little older, but basically nothing and nobody had changed. Except me. Somehow I didn't quite belong any more.

I'd forgotten how green it all was, and how dirty the cities were, weighed down with dust of centuries. I'd lost my ear for the regional dialects and I had totally forgotten the niceties of English afternoon tea, the nuances of which made my Edmonton tea parties look very brash.

Once I accepted this it didn't take me long to fit in again. But Bryan was a different matter. He was an out and out Canadian and embarrassed me on several occasions by passing remarks in a tone of voice that left no one in any doubt that he didn't reckon much to the English way of doing things. Even the London underground didn't meet fully with his approval.

"Why didn't that guy shout, all aboard?" he asked loudly.

He terrified my aunts with what they called "his wild west games," and obviously was not considered a very good influence on his cousins. One day my aunt rushed in from the garden.

"Your young westerner is on the top of the garden steps brandishing a knife," she spluttered.

English children apparently did not brandish carving knives when playing at hunting.

I tried not to disrupt the different houses where we visited but it was not easy. Fortunately, we kept moving. I'd one wonderful break when Dr. and Mrs. Percy Backus, of Dagenham, invited me to visit them. The Backuses had lived in Alberta in the early settlement years, but had returned to England to allow their sons to attend medical school.

Dr. Backus took us under his wing, and it didn't take him long to sum up our situation. He said I must have a day away from Bryan and Bryan must have a day in which to express himself.

Glory be!

No one has ever said I missed an opportunity, and I certainly wasn't going to miss this one. I arranged to go into London with Mrs. Backus. Barry, their son, took a day off his studies and offered to look after Bryan. I had a wonderful day. Poor Barry told me that although he played Rugby football regularly, it was not as strenuous as the day he'd spent in the garden with Bryan.

Despite this, my young Albertan didn't put them off Canadians. Both the sons, Dr. Barry and Dr. Winston Backus, returned to the Prairies and opened a medical office in Ponoka. Later, Winston Backus became the Minister of Public Works in the Alberta Government. Their parents, Dr. Percy and his wife, still make frequent visits to Canada and we always have a happy reunion. Heaven help us! Dr. Percy Backus is over ninety years old, and I'm eighty-five — that's one friendship that has spanned a good long time.

The year 1938 was a strange time to be paying my first visit back to my birthland. All the time I was in England rumors of war filled the air. I had forgotten the English habit of compressing news into one succinct phrase on a board outside the news agent's store and really panicked when I read on a board: "England Declares." My heart flipped. "The war; it's started! How am I going to get back to Canada?"

I need not have panicked. The sign was referring to cricket.

The London undergrounds were incredibly noisy, not from people and trains but from pneumatic drills, saws and pick axes, and there was a haze of construction dust in the air. The official explanation was that the stations were being enlarged, but you cannot pull the wool over the eyes of the British man on the street.

On every side I was told, "That's nonsense. The Government is building subterranean air-raid shelters to protect the people from bombs."

They were right.

One of my relatives held a position in Somerset House, home of many of Britain's official records. He came home one day and confidentially told me all the records had been moved to a secret place in another part of England. It was at this time Mr. Chamberlain and his umbrella went over to see Mr. Hitler in Munich. Chamberlain came back showing a full set of teeth and proclaiming all was well; Hitler had assured him of peace in our time. This didn't fool anyone I met, and all continued to make plans for the war.

Harry was still going ahead with arrangements in Canada. Mother was not able to talk, but by writing notes she could communicate slowly. She was obviously looking forward to the visit to England and the doctor thought it would do her good to have a holiday. The gloom and doom over the impending war obviously had not yet extended to the Commonwealth.

Eventually I received a telegram, and the Backus family drove Bryan and me down to Southampton docks to meet them. Mother looked well despite her inability to speak, but the sight of her upset me. I couldn't help but think of the time she came to Canada and Dad couldn't stand her chattering. Now, because of his death she had lost her voice.

Dr. Percy Backus was wonderful to our family. After our happy reunion, he took Mother under his wing and whisked her away to stay with her niece in Brighton. I remember being very impressed when, on a trip to see that Mother was safely installed, Barry hit 100 miles an hour on a good stretch of road. It was an incredible speed to those of us used to the roads in western Canada.

Dr. Percy Backus looked after Mother very carefully. I have no idea what kind of treatment he used, but by the time she returned from her long visit in Brighton she could speak again and the trauma seemed almost healed. The trip to England was worth every penny we spent on it.

Harry was as surprised as I had been when he heard the rumors about the war. Even the barrowboys selling their wares on the street corners used the impending disaster to sell goods.

As we passed a barrow heaped with towels and tablecloths, the owner leaped out and almost rubbed our faces in the washcloths he was trying to peddle. When we refused to buy them, he shook his head sadly.

"Yer'll be sorry. Yer'll be beggin' for 'em soon."

How right he was. The English housewife couldn't get anything like that during the war, and some did have to beg for them and then pay through the nose on the black market.

Once Mother could speak again she was happy to contact all her old friends and do the social round. One of her exceedingly proper friends had a home by the sea at Bridlington. She invited Harry, myself and Bryan to visit her for two days, but before she made the final commitment met us for a meal at the Station Hotel. She obviously wanted to check us out and see if we were still socially acceptable after twenty years in the wild west.

We obviously passed the acid test. After a sumptuous meal Mrs. Telford-Swanson said her "man" would call for us in four days' time.

I was delighted. I envisioned Bryan at last being able to run off his energy on the beach and build sand castles to his heart's content.

Four days later we were ready and waiting for the car to arrive. I had not thought out the implication of having a "man" and was horrified when a huge limousine, driven by a pompous-looking individual in a chauffeur's uniform, glided sedately to a halt in front of us. Poor Bryan. This obviously wasn't going to be the carefree time I had hoped for. We sat uncomfortably on the edge of our seats and I was terrified that Bryan was going to resort to his baser instincts and tip the chauffeur's cap over his eyes.

As our hostess had been endowed with money and not children, Bryan set out to entertain her. Walking into the massive hall he cocked a thumb at a priceless bronze statue and asked, "Hey, who's that guy on horseback?" With a shudder, Mrs. Telford-Swanson said, "Napoleon."

Undaunted, Bryan continued to look around. Catching a glimpse of her "man" in the garden, he said, "Do you know the cab driver has not gone home yet?" He was a past master at embarrassing us, and my pleas of "No Bryan" were a constant refrain.

Those were the longest two days of my life. Finally the visit ended and we breezed out of the house and down to the Bridlington harbor.

There among the seething hordes of holidaymakers we bought fish and chips wrapped in newspapers. We ate them with our fingers while paddling in the waves with our shoes and socks hanging around our necks. I could almost see Mrs. Telford-Swanson shuddering.

Eventually our holiday was over and we sailed away from Southampton with heavy hearts, wondering how long it would be before we saw our relatives and friends again. But despite the parting from the land of our birth we were happy to be going home. The land of our adoption had become very dear to us and we felt that was where we truly belonged.

Our trip to England had indeed been what the doctor had ordered, and both Mother and I were ready to pick up our responsibilities again. But the parting would have been more traumatic if we had all realized that the dreaded Holocaust was not an imaginary scare tactic but would come to pass, and we would never again see the old England and many dear friends.

21
Visitors

While in England we had thrown out invitations to all and sundry. "Come and visit us in Alberta" seemed a fairly safe and hospitable thing to say, as we assumed most people just didn't have the wherewithal to take us up on our offer. We should have known better.

We had been back in Alberta only a few months, when out of the blue a cable arrived from Mother's cousin, Winnifred Blanchard. Winnifred was coming to visit us.

My heart sank. We were just settling down into our new routine after our visit to England. Mother was able, with help, to return to her own apartment at the store. I was back to my usual bubbly self, and Harry and Bryan were contented and happy.

I didn't really want to disrupt things, and if ever there was a disruptive force it was our Winnifred.

Winnifred arrived fast on the heels of her telegram. Tall, full bosomed and well corseted, and dressed in the latest fashions, she shook us rigid with her first pronouncements.

"I've heard there are a lot of men over here," she stated with her British feet planted firmly in the middle of my kitchen. "So I'm going to stay until I get married again."

Winnifred was sixty.

Harry never said a word but went silently into the bedroom. When I went to find him a little later I was surprised to see him solemnly making a list. On it were all the elderly bachelors we knew. "Just speeding up the process," he explained.

We all knew that Britain ruled the waves — or thought she did — but Winnifred ruled every kitchen she had ever stepped into. Mine was no exception and she immediately took us over. Mind you, as far as my kitchen was concerned she could have it. I thankfully handed over lock, stock and icebox, and let her go to it.

This was a fatal mistake, and I nearly screamed when I received her first grocery list. It was headed up by a long list of dried fruits — only the best brands specified. Winnifred had decided to make our Christmas cakes. This was in the heat of July! Explaining forcefully that we should be honored as she had been given the recipe straight from the royal household, she overruled my protests and we sweltered for two days until the oven cooled down.

We didn't have the royal purse, but I must confess that our Christmas cakes that year were super. Admitting that aloud, though, was the wrong thing to do. Winnifred looked down her nose in surprise and said, "Of course I'm noted for my wonderful cakes."

Winnifred soon reorganized our home. It became so tidy with everything in a place of its own that I felt quite out of place. Even my canning jars were lined up and sparkling on a shelf instead of huddled together in a box. But I would not let her attack the store and that was a constant source of irritation to her.

Mother and Winnifred did not get on; even as young girls there had been tension between them. Mother took one look at the way

103

she was reorganizing me and threatened to shut up the shop and pull down the blinds if Winnifred as much as set foot on the sidewalk.

The only way to get rid of her seemed to be to fall in with her plans and marry her off, so I diligently searched for a man. Unfortunately our circle was short of unattached senior widowers or bachelors. I would willingly have bought the ingredients for her three-tiered wedding cake, which I'm sure she would have made with her royal recipe. But no such luck.

One day Winnifred let slip that she had a friend in Vancouver. This was our chance. Waxing eloquent about the number of unattached males who littered the shoreline, we coaxed her to hop on a train and pay a visit to Vancouver. Winnifred departed, waving a fond goodbye and assuring us she'd "soon be back."

The dust had no sooner settled than another cable arrived from England. This one announced that Dan Soper would be paying us a visit en route to British Columbia. We began to get very neurotic about cables.

Dan was the musical conductor of a London orchestra. We'd met him in London, found him delightful company and issued our usual invitation.

Fortunately Dan was a different type of guest than Winnifred. Arriving two days after we'd waved her off, he had his itinerary completely mapped out.

He assured us he was only stopping over a few days in Edmonton. Then he would move on to Banff to start his tour of the Rockies.

His one request was to see something "truly western." Harry wracked his brains, then hit upon the idea of driving out to spend the weekend at Wainwright Park. This was the last bastion of the herds of buffalo that once roamed the prairies. Buffalo and elk herds freely wandered the park and it was the nearest and biggest stretch of bald prairie. This thrilled Dan. He was excited about "stalwart men and mighty beasts."

We had planned to spend the Saturday night at the Wainwright Hotel, a primitive spot but the only accommodation. We needn't have worried; Dan was in his element. This was the stuff the Hollywood westerns were made of, as far as he was concerned, and we had great difficulty persuading him not to walk off with one of the brass spittoons scattered around the foyer.

Of course, seen through his eyes it was indeed like an old western, with the local cowboys in their plaid shirts, and the native Indians rolling their cigarettes with one hand while leaning nonchalantly across the bar. As he sat tensely on the edge of his seat, he hoped a cowboy would slam through the doors with both guns blazing. We couldn't have pleased him more if we had tried, "It's so truly western," he kept whispering to Harry.

Sunday morning we had breakfast and planned to return home. Tucking into another "truly western" tradition, pancakes and syrup, we were brought rudely back to reality by a radio announcement. Crackling out of the ether came a stunning message to the whole world. Neville Chamberlain, the Prime Minister of England, announced, "Poland has been invaded and England has declared war."

There was total silence in the dining room as the meaning of the catastrophe sunk in. This was "it." I turned to Dan, concerned he would be stranded in Canada. With all the arrogance of the British abroad, he assured me that Britain would soon have everything under control.

I was not so easily convinced. The next day I persuaded Dan to go to the travel agent to book a passage back to England. I insisted on a copy of his itinerary so that I would know where he was on the Atlantic. We said farewell to Dan and, sad to say, we never met him again.

War was the signal for Winnifred to return from B.C. Unfortunately, she hadn't got her man.

The news of the declaration of war had rocked her. Her first thought was that she would stay in Canada "for the duration." On second thought, she decided that this was not such a good idea; her three children would all be in the war zone.

Her eldest son was in the guards, her daughter a nursing sister, and her youngest son on an aircraft carrier. All would be involved with the fighting. It was a mother's dilemma and she didn't know whether to go back to her home in the north of England, or stay in safety in Canada. We sympathized. Having been in England the year before, we felt a close bond with our families and friends there.

Finally she made up her mind. She would return to England as soon as possible. My fertile brain began to perk. Dan would be boarding his ship in two weeks time, and I knew the sailing time. Why not book Winnifred on the same voyage, and then we would only have one crossing to worry about? These two had never met, but Winnifred could soon check with the purser and they could look after each other.

We went out and managed to get the last berth on that ship.

Despite the trouble she had caused us, it was with a sad heart that we bade our relative farewell. War immediately played havoc with the mail service, and once the ship had sailed we had no news of the travellers for weeks.

Eventually a letter did come from Winnifred. She had successfully met up with Dan, but that was the only pleasant thing that happened on the voyage. The crossing was dreadful. Although part of a convoy, they had been chased by submarines and the journey had taken much longer than anticipated. The passengers wore their life belts constantly, and not only were they uncomfortable, but the perpetual fear of being torpedoed meant no one slept very much.

Dan and Winnifred really did get to know each other. When they finally arrived safely in England, Dan invited Winnifred to become his housekeeper in London. "A-ha!" I thought "Winnifred has got her man."

Possibly romance would have blossomed, but Hitler started his bombardment of London and she fled in panic to her home up in the north.

She should have stayed in London. Mr. Hitler followed her and took the front wall of her house out in an air raid.

Luckily Winnifred was saved by being in a shelter. She took it all very well. She wrote and told us she had always fancied having the centre wall of her house knocked down to make one big living room like our Canadian houses had. She just hadn't envisioned it happening quite so suddenly.

Winnifred's three children all survived the hostilities, but she never remarried. She and Dan never met again. He was killed in an air raid, and she, too, died before the war was over.

22
Moving To Vancouver

The war was getting me down. The constant worry about family and friends made everyone we knew harassed and short-tempered. We weren't helped by feeling guilty about it. Knowing how bad the English situation was made our life in Alberta seem relatively trouble free. Yet the constant bad news and shortages on imported items, coupled with the usual Alberta weather, made life a constant hassle.

"Wouldn't it be nice," I grumbled to Harry, "if we could leave cold Alberta and continue our love affair with the coast?"

Although my remark had been idly uttered, the idea took root. I was tired of struggling with Alberta winters. It was a ridiculous climate to try and survive in, so why bother? We loved the coast, had made many friends there, and the temperature never dropped much below freezing. Why live at 40 below when you don't have to?

Harry argued that our roots were now deeply embedded in Alberta and it would be difficult for him to find as good a job in B.C. I persuaded him that despite his misgivings we would all be much happier in Vancouver.

Once his mind was made up, Harry moved fast. In no time at all he and I were in Vancouver, house hunting. He astounded the real estate man by announcing, "This will do. We'll buy it" — "it" being the very first house we were shown.

The agent was horrified. He wanted to make some pretence of earning his commission. Couldn't he show us at least two more houses? We could always come back to the first one.

Harry insisted. He'd made up his mind and was ready to sign the papers.

"But don't you want to beat them down on the price?" asked the bewildered man.

"No," said Harry firmly, and pulled out his pen. "I cannot afford to argue as I've only a small amount of cash for a down payment, and I want easy terms."

I think the man made a little notation in his book: "Prairie suckers."

The agent didn't realize that Harry worked on hunches. As soon as we walked into the front door, Harry knew it was a good property.

It was certainly a spectacular spot. Well situated on English Bay, it was an old mansion that had been built in more opulent times by a successful gold miner. No expense had been spared, and it had certainly been built to last.

Sitting solidly on fortress-like foundations, its fifteen rooms fanned out from a large central hallway that featured a parquet floor, cathedral-like stained-glass windows, and a curved oak stairway which gracefully climbed to a minstrel gallery on the second floor. I was captivated by the minstrel gallery and Harry struck by the beautiful windows, but Bryan couldn't wait to slide down the banisters or swing from a rope on the balcony.

The rest of the house was equally spectacular. All the bathrooms were marble (except for the ones in the servants' quarters). The massive kitchen could hold an army of servants and even boasted a butler's pantry, and thank goodness the whole house was linked by an intercom system of speaking tubes.

The house stood on a corner and should have looked straight down the street to the Crystal Pool and the sea beyond, but the original owner had planted small Douglas firs that had grown as tall as their friends in Stanley Park. They completely blocked the view, and gave the house a depressing and forbidding appearance.

"We'll have to hack that lot down," I stated firmly. I was used to bush, but nothing quite of this dimension.

We signed the agreement of sale and gave the resident family a possession date of several months ahead. This would allow us time to sort out our life back in Alberta, raise the extra cash and sell our property.

Cash was to be our main concern, but we had high hopes. We still owned our homestead land up in the north and were confident that its sale would give us the funds we needed.

Shock number one hit when the homestead quarter section sold for only $700. Then the hay section went for $500. This, of course, was before the real estate commission was extracted. I couldn't believe the land brought us so little; we had probably paid more in its taxes over the last twenty-five years.

We had no difficulty at all selling our local west end home. We asked $3500 and got $3000, though, this didn't make up for the loss on the homestead, and once again we found ourselves scraping the bottom of the barrel. I was beginning to feel that it was a wonder the old barrel had any bottom left. Still our hopes were far from blighted, and we were ready to face a new adventure. Even Mother seemed ready to adapt, especially to the prospect of a much milder winter.

All that was left now was for Harry to submit his resignation to the courts.

He would hand it in personally, not mail it. This decision got me in a dreadful mess.

The Attorney-General was very friendly with Harry. He was convinced we were making a mistake in moving to the coast.

"Harry, have you thought this out clearly?"

Harry assured him that we had. We'd already purchased a house there and we needed a change.

The Attorney-General thought about this for a while, then tore up Harry's resignation and made a counter offer.

"Look Harry, I think you are making a big mistake, and we certainly cannot afford to lose you in the Supreme Court. I want you to consider taking a six months leave of absence, with three months pay. If at the end of your leave you come back, your job will be waiting. But this must be kept strictly confidential."

This was an offer we couldn't refuse.

Naturally, many of my friends had court connections, so it was more than my life was worth even to hint at what the Attorney-General had told Harry. I therefore had to go the rounds of the farewell showers with everyone thinking we were well and truly burning our boats. This "keep it strictly confidential" hung over me like the sword of Damocles.

Every time we found ourselves at a farewell party being showered with gifts and good wishes, I found myself biting my tongue in order to stop screaming, "Please, no more! We just might be back."

Eventually, the four of us travelled to Vancouver by train. We shipped all our worldly goods, including the piano, to arrive at the house on our possession date. Among ourselves we already called this new house "The Gables," for like our homestead it had gabled windows on its upper floor.

Having a few days to spare before taking possession, we deposited Mother with acquaintances of hers in Vancouver, and our small family visited the Fraser Valley to stay with our old friends the Peacocks.

We managed to enroll Bryan in the local school in the valley, just on a temporary basis. Large numbers of Japanese-Canadian children were enrolled here too. The government was beginning to move great numbers of people of Japanese heritage to internment camps on the prairies. History has recorded this forced migration to the interior, which shows how innocent people suffer in senseless wars.

The weather was perfect and we enjoyed golfing and fishing with our friends. Just as we were thinking of leaving, we received notice of an auction due to take place in the new house the day before we moved in. We decided to attend.

This was the signal for the weather to change. The day we bussed into Vancouver the heavens opened; like an omen of doom, the driving rain and glowering skies pressed down upon us and took all the joy out of our adventure. We eventually arrived on the doorstep of the Big House, wet to the skin and with our spirits at a low ebb.

Masses of raincoated people, pools of water and dripping umbrellas met us in the beautiful hall. The air was thick with the odor of steamy wet clothing, and I felt as though I were standing in an overcrowded steam bath.

A large number of depressed-looking people were hunched together in the livingroom, like old hens in the chicken house. The auctioneer made a fine rooster as he crowed over the articles to be auctioned from his perch on the top of a fine oak table.

He crowed in vain. No matter how much he jollied them along, the public was not in a buying mood. They stood around soggily and were obviously loathe to part with any cash. Actually I think they had only come in to shelter from the rain.

We had attended this sale hoping to bid on some furniture. We knew the items we had shipped would not go very far in this enormous mansion. Realizing there wasn't much opposition we cheered up and bid happily on a few items.

Suddenly a lady pushed through the crowd. "You're the Holmeses," she cried. "Remember me? Gladys Smalley; you stayed at my place on Cordova Street some years ago."

I didn't remember her at all at first, but as she continued talking I had faint glimmering of a landlady who was hard on Bryan and made us line up for the bathroom. I'd disliked her then and she wasn't doing anything for me now.

It turned out Gladys was now doing some kind of war work and was about to clock in on duty. In no time flat she organized us to bid on some items of furniture for her. This was a nuisance but somehow we were talked into it. As she swung herself around to leave she cast her eye about the house and delivered her parting shot.

"I don't know who was daft enough to buy this old dump, but it will need a fortune to put it right, let alone keep it up."

I stood in my puddle and felt all the ginger drain right out of me.

As things turned out, Gladys missed her chance. Discouraged by the lack of response the auctioneer picked up his hammer and prepared to depart. I stopped him.

"What about all this junk that's left?"

"Oh, you can have it," he said.

"But what about the mess?" I wailed.

"Oh, the new owners will clean up," he tossed over his shoulder. And he splashed out with the grey people following silently behind.

Harry and I sat on the bottom step of the once beautiful staircase, and I cried buckets of tears that were just absorbed by the mud. For once, Harry's hug and standby comment — "come on, it could be worse" — held no comfort. I wasn't sure it could.

23
Taking Up Residence

A week after the auction it was still raining cats and dogs. The rain was obviously a dire and dreadful warning but we took no notice, hoping the ominous feelings it aroused would go away. No such luck. Our problems never stopped from the day we took possession.

The door chimes echoed through the house. There on the doorstep stood a sad-looking young woman with a baby in her arms, and another small child hanging on to her skirts.

"Have you some rooms to rent?" she asked, tiredly.

Heavens, I'd lots of rooms, but we had been warned not to rent them out. Because of the wartime situation, a Federal renters' protection act was in full force, an act which protected lodgers from losing their rooms. This was of course commendable, but had unfortunate consequences for us. If we let rooms, it would be impossible to get the people out.

What a quandary to be in. I felt so sorry for this homeless woman and we could have done with the rent money, but what if we decided to go back to Alberta in a few months and couldn't get rid of our lodgers?

Regretfully I shook my head.

Immediately this meek-looking woman turned into a termagant, railing against rich people having big houses and being so selfish.

Horrified, I quickly shut the front door. I heard sobs from the poor young woman, and leaning against the inside of the door burst into tears myself. Harry arrived home and found me weeping as though my heart would break as I sat on my old friend, the bottom stair. I implored him to answer the door in future. If this was a sample of the calls we could expect, I couldn't face it.

To take my mind off this unpleasant incident, I set out on a tour of discovery. I needed to poke around and become familiar

Peggy and Harry out for a drive in their
Model-T Ford with their dog Buster on
the fender.

Lewis's Confectionary Store on 124th St.
and 107 Ave. was run for years by
Peggy's mother and father.

The Gables — Peggy's "dream house" built on 125 St.

Inside The Gables — showing the Jacobean tea table before Peggy sawed off the legs!

The cold Christmas party at Cromdale Hall. Harry is in the back row, second from right. Peggy is in the front row, third from right.

Madame Victoria Nurkse visiting Peggy and Bryan. Despite her efforts, Bryan never did sing!

Harry teaching Bryan how to fish at Bow Falls, Banff, 1935.

Peggy and Bryan pose for a formal portrait about 1938.

with every nook and cranny of our new abode. Finding the basement steps in what looked like a cupboard, down I ventured.

Harry didn't need the intercom to hear my piercing screams. He belted down the stairs to find me, a heap of jelly, crouched down by the furnace and gazing horrified into a dark recess.

"What in the name of God have you seen?"

I pointed with a shaking finger. There rising from the floor was a strange head. White and ghostly it gazed right back at us, its neck emerging from the concrete floor.

Harry drew his breath sharply, then bravely he went over and bent down. I shut my eyes as I was sure something horrid was going to happen; then I heard him laugh.

Opening my eyes slowly I saw him pick the head up. Made of plaster, it had obviously been used in shop windows to display hats. No one had told me that the daughter of the previous owners had run a boutique.

After my fright I declared I wasn't going down in the basement in future without him but since he was already there maybe it was a good time to acquaint ourselves with the furnace.

Crouched in the middle of our basement with tentacles uplifted and forcing themselves into every room, the furnace looked like a malevolent octopus. It was obviously very hungry. We set a small fire in its gaping maw, and the wood was consumed almost as quickly as we could feed it in. This had no effect on the frigid temperature of the house.

Obviously this furnace would rapidly consume whatever we could throw in, and unfortunately we had nothing other than rubbish with which to feed it. Fuel would have to become our first priority. Happy to have a job I could handle, I set out to look for a fuel man.

Armed with a list from our friends, I called on every supplier, but in vain. Didn't I know there was a war on and we should have been registered?

I pleaded. How could we have registered when we didn't know at the outbreak we were going to move? This made not one jot of difference. According to the city there was nothing — no coal, no sawdust to damp it down and make it last, no wood.

The cold, damp Vancouver air was very penetrating.

After many journeys, I eventually found someone who would supply us. He was a bootlegger, of course. Every time someone ordered fourteen bags of coal, he received only the true equivalent of thirteen. Lucky people like ourselves bought the extra bag at double the price, but at least it enabled us to get a little warmer.

Our front-door chimes were never silent. The more activity there was with the coal deliveries and a stream of workmen, the more people came hopefully to the door requesting lodgings. Sooner or later we were bound to give in, especially as Harry could not find a job and we needed some cash to keep going.

Our weak moment came in the form of Harvey.

Harvey was a nice-looking young man. He too wanted to rent an apartment but he had a different story. The apartment was needed not for himself but for his parents. They lived in Provost, Alberta, and wanted to spend the winter months in Vancouver. Could they lodge with us?

Harry explained our position. Harvey understood our plight but thought it might be to our advantage to rent to his parents. They only wanted it for the winter months; they would have to return in the spring to sow the new crops.

If we could let them have a couple of rooms Harvey would promise they would be out by April or May.

We were obviously weakening, so Harvey added the final touch. Looking around at our somewhat decrepit mansion, he explained his father was very handy and hated time hanging on his hands. How would we like some help to fix up the house?

That settled it.

The Bostik family was definitely sent from heaven. Mr. and Mrs. Bostik were a delight, and Mr. Bostik was incredibly handy. He advised us what to do to remodel the old house and did many of the jobs himself. In fact we all became firm friends.

One day, Harry and Mr. Bostik were faced with a real problem. The fireplace chimney in one of the upstairs bedrooms was completely blocked. They poked and prodded to no avail and eventually had to call in the chimney sweep.

The sweep tried all the tricks that he knew, including peppering the obstruction with shot by firing a gun up the chimney, an exercise that terrified me and covered us all with soot. Eventually he had to admit he was nonplussed.

Consultants were brought in, and finally after much huffing and puffing and chipping away, the cause was discovered. Some previous occupant of that room had obviously been a secret drinker, and disposed of the bottles up the chimney.

Gradually over the years the heat of the fires had caused the glass to melt and seal the flue. No wonder the chimney sweep couldn't get his brush up.

We had to demolish part of the chimney completely, then rebuild it.

Soon after his parents were well settled, Harvey asked if he could move in with them. How could we refuse? Harvey joined us all and once more we were lucky. His proved to be another set of helpful hands and brains.

Strange things were happening in Vancouver at this time. Because of the war shortages, everyone was buying things on the black market and trying not to get caught. Sometimes the phone would ring about midnight.

"Harry?" a ghostly voice would whisper, "can you come over quickly with your shovel? They've just dumped my load of sawdust on the boulevard and I have to get it shifted before morning."

Lucky them, to have a load of sawdust at all.

Because of the fuel shortages, we had lined up all the old basket furniture left from the auction. It was ready to feed into the furnace in case of emergency.

In going through the junk in the basement we found plenty of things we could burn, but also some very expensive equipment including a full outfit for mountaineering, interesting bits and bridles from someone's horse-riding days, and lots of old pottery. Then came the big find: a dilapidated old box, stuffed under some moth-eaten carpets. Our eyes bulged in complete disbelief when dragging it to the light we discovered it contained $150,000 worth of gold shares.

We didn't know what to do with them so Harry took one and made discreet inquiries. Unfortunately they turned out to be worthless, but Bryan had a wonderful time playing with them.

Gradually we began to make the place habitable and Mother

moved in with us. Just before Christmas the rain stopped but the snows came.

Everyone said it was the worst weather in forty years, but that was cold comfort to me.

The only person who didn't mind the snow was Bryan. Skating happily on the lagoon and building snowmen, he thoroughly enjoyed himself. The rest of us froze. When I went into the lounge to play my piano, I wore my gloves and winter-lined snowboots.

One day I had a great burst of creative energy. The dark oak panelling on the main floor was getting me down. I dashed downtown and bought some beautiful dogwood wallpaper. Papering the wall over the fireplace in the lounge cheered me up immediately. For there, ignoring the dank weather outside, were the beautiful spring blossoms of the dogwood. The whole house brightened.

I suspect that later owners would curse me when peeling it off, and wonder what idiot had wallpapered over such beautiful oak panelling.

Vancouver in wartime was very different from the carefree city we knew from happy holidays. The docks were sealed off from the public, and the harbor full of camouflaged ships at anchor. All was poised, ready and waiting for the call to action.

I had always loved the English Bay area of Vancouver and so had Harry. This was one of the reasons he had made up his mind so quickly when buying our mansion.

To our disgust, now people spoke of English Bay as "the slum district" and despaired of its ever returning to its former glory and social status. Comments like this made me feel as though we were living on the wrong side of the tracks. We certainly seemed to have bought in the wrong district or at the wrong time. All around us elegant houses were falling into decay for lack of money to keep them up, and we were struggling to keep our own property in order.

"This is the end of English Bay," said one pessimistic person. "They'll have to demolish all this lot by the time the bums have finished living here."

How wrong they all were. If only we'd a crystal ball to see into the future. English Bay is now back to its former glory, and I wish, oh how I wish, we still owned our beautiful mansion.

24
Remuddling!

Half of Vancouver was homeless at this time, and it seemed that every person wanted to lodge with us. Each time workmen appeared at our home, people assumed we were converting into suites and another onslaught on the doorbell would begin.

Despite our resolve not to get into any tricky situations, occasionally we would be worn down by individual plights, and rent out a room on a temporary basis. But I never stopped feeling vulnerable when handing over a key to a stranger, and I always worried if he didn't come in at night.

National Housing phoned one day and asked if we had a single room for a young airman. I was quite excited. Here was our chance to do something for the war effort. That would please Harry.

Harry and other veterans of the first war were feeling ignored and ill-treated by the recruiting policies of this war. It seemed as though anyone over the age of thirty was over the hill as far as serving his country was concerned. The veterans would some-times gather on a viewpoint overlooking the docks. While they watched the activity centring around the war ships at anchor, the men would relive the old campaigns and past glories from "their war" and swap the latest news of the Battle of Britain.

Having an airman with us would be a wonderful chance for Harry to get some of the latest information on the fighting. But I was concerned about the boy's comfort; after all, airmen must get their rest.

Our only spare bed was a lumpy old mattress on the floor in

one of the many ex-servants' rooms. I knew Harry wouldn't want someone who might cause Hitler's demise to be sleeping on the floor, so I rushed out to buy a new bed. The only one I could find was a collapsing cot, but it was well sprung and certainly seemed better than the old mattress.

The airman was a cheerful young fellow of about eighteen with a shock of bright red hair, a wide grin and a smart uniform. He assured me he was glad of anything to sleep on, so I showed him to his room and turned to go.

I had just started down the stairs when there was a terrific crash. I burst back into the room to find the bed folded up like a sandwich with the airman inside. All that was visible were two feet and a hand flailing around wildly. I didn't like to hold the airman's hand in case he thought I was getting fresh, so I grabbed his foot and pulled. There was a muffled yelp of agony. I'd pulled the leg that was firmly pinched by the folding mechanism.

No matter where I pulled on the bed I couldn't unfasten it. The airman's weight pushed firmly on the hinge. Harry was out and my neighbor next door at work. There was only one thing I could do. I attacked the bed with a screwdriver.

The screws were very stiff but I persevered, and gradually a pile of nuts appeared beside me. Suddenly the whole bed fell to pieces and the airman was able to extract himself from the remains. He took it very well and helped me sort out the bits of bed and fit them together. Unfortunately, there were one or two pieces that didn't seem to go anywhere, and in the crash I seemed to have mislaid a couple of screws.

We tried to tie the bed up with wire but it seemed distinctly shaky, so the airman stacked the frame in the corner and spread the mattress out on, you've guessed it, the floor.

Another airman who stayed with us was so used to flying he couldn't sleep unless he felt high off the ground. To help him we not only resurrected the collapsing cot but added a teetering layer of cushions to bolster the height. Each night Harry and I would heave this lump of a kid up on top; then he slept like a lamb. They never talk about this kind of war effort in the history books.

After the airmen, an elderly man took over the room. He was

118

the only lodger we had to ask to leave. It was a pity for he was a nice old man. Unfortunately he would cook bacon in his room in the middle of the night. This wouldn't have been so awful, except that he used a blowtorch.

Each day the cold and damp seemed to intensify and seep a little further into my bones. Bryan kept warm by tying a rope to the balcony railings, launching himself into the air, and swinging across the hallway to the accompaniment of wild whoops and cries.

He always seemed to be doing this when a prospective tenant arrived, and sometimes their shrieks as Bryan hurtled earthward, rivalled his. Their reactions to our young Tarzan always gave me a clue to their personalities. Harry called it part of the screening process.

I got increasingly disillusioned with the whole move to the coast, especially as I knew it was my bright idea that had us all there. Harry tried to distract me from our worries and took me out to a movie. Unfortunately it was How Green Was My Valley, and I sobbed all the way through.

Our new friends decided to prove Vancouver wasn't really as bad as I thought. They got together with Harry and organized an enormous surprise party for me.

In order to have a roaring fire for the guests, Harry cut down the stand of Douglas firs that blocked our view. At last it was possible to look at the sea — if it would ever stop raining and the fog lift.

The party was an incredible success. For a while everyone forgot there was a war on. The tables groaned with the mass of food. I couldn't believe the array of wonderful dishes. It seemed everyone had hoarded a few favorite delicacies for just such an occasion.

Cheering me up was the excuse, but actually everyone was ready for a break, and for a few short hours we all forgot our troubles.

It was certainly a return to the good old days. The fire roared up the chimneys and glimmered on the oak panelling. Music, laughter and merriment rang through the house. I hadn't realized how many friends we'd acquired. The whole neighborhood came. Everyone brought a piece of fuel to ram into the furnace, which roared and pumped out hot air like a dragon. Not satisfied with this I recklessly heaped the remains of the Douglas firs on the fireplace till it crackled and glowed and roared up the chimney in the lounge, throwing out so much heat no one could bear to stand in front of it. Sweat beaded the men's foreheads, but I didn't care. For the first time since arriving in Vancouver, we were warm.

Our good time lasted until the guests departed. Then, surveying the mess and feeling the damp chill creeping back into the house, I had a strong urge to walk into the ocean. But as always my common sense asserted itself. I came to my senses and decided I would look for a job. I might have more luck than Harry.

The employment bureau didn't help my self-image. Looking at me over her steel-rimmed glasses, a grey-haired woman told me disapprovingly I was too old for anything. The fact I was years younger than she was obviously didn't strike her. I walked mournfully back to our mansion.

I decided the only thing to do was throw myself back into the hard work of remodelling — or remuddling, as Harry called it — the house, and resolved to tackle the part that I hated most, the kitchen.

Built in the days when armies of servants were a normal part of a rich household, the kitchen would have held a platoon. The floor, like a small acreage, spread in front of me. Covered with the grime of ages the original color of the linoleum was totally obscured. From the cavernous ceiling, an enormous array of hardwood slats, ropes and pulleys glowered over me. This was supposed to be the arrangement for drying clothes, but it looked like a medieval instrument of torture.

Down on my knees I went, with a pail of soapy water and a knife to chip off the caked grease. I rolled up my sleeves and attacked the floor with gusto. Suddenly there was a creak and groan and I saw stars. The ropes above me had given way and the whole wooden drying contraption came down on my head.

Funnily enough this seemed to knock some sense into my head. My life flashed before me. What on earth was I doing scrubbing a stupid kitchen floor in war-torn Vancouver?

I'd been running away.

The moment of truth hit me with the clothes drier.

No wonder I had been depressed and restless. I was going through a change of life, not only physically but emotionally I was rebelling against the social structures in which I had become trapped.

Edmonton was home, but the social life I had been living there was stunting me. I wasn't a tea party socialite; I was a woman with a mind of her own and a lot of creative abilities. It was time for me to use them.

I never did find out that color of the kitchen linoleum. That night as Harry came in I threw my arms around his neck, apologized for causing such a disruption to the family, and told him I was ready to go back to Edmonton if he wanted to take up the Attorney-General's offer and resume his old job again.

I will draw a blank over Harry's reply. He'd grown quite fond of Vancouver.

25
Deadline For Departure

Everyone has made silly decisions, but I truly earned whatever was the forties' equivalent of the Turkey of the Year Award when I persuaded my family to move to Vancouver. I paid the penalty for the deed when we tried to sell our mansion and pick up the pieces back in Edmonton. Nothing seemed to proceed smoothly, and we went from crisis to crisis until I thought my head would never stop spinning.

Once again a For Sale sign went up in the front yard. What optimism we had. No one in his right mind would buy our enormous mansion in such times of economic hardship. The rose-colored glasses had fallen from my eyes and I saw Vancouver as it really was in the war-torn forties, not as I had remembered it from the sunshine years of the twenties.

I had always dreamed of living in Vancouver. During the long bleak prairie winters of our homesteading years I had fantasized about the primroses and sunshine at the coast. Every holiday we had taken there reinforced that image of balmy breezes, sunshine, sand and glittering water all framed by spectacular mountains. To me, Vancouver had everything.

It was hard to abandon a dream and come to terms with reality. During the war years, Vancouver was far from a dream. It was a grey city: grey people, grey ships, grey weather. The Depression had taken its toll, and poverty and hardship lined many faces. Everyone looked, and probably was, permanently cold.

Once-elegant houses, boarded up and empty, lined streets filled with passersby who had no home. Stanley Park was a horrific prison for Japanese-Canadians, and the English Bay beach, once a beauty spot, was unspeakable. Covered with garbage, filthy oil and grease, it was washed by tides that threw up even more refuse from the ships in the bay.

This was the area in which we were hoping to attract a buyer. Needless to say, no one came rushing up our front path except real estate men hoping to persuade us to list with them.

Before we had fully discussed what we were going to do if we couldn't sell, the door chimes pealed. There on the step was Galdys Smalley, the bustling landlady who had been so scathing at the auction just before we moved in.

"Trust her to be in at the kill," I thought as I stood poised and ready to shut the door. I assumed that she had appeared to try and buy our furniture at rock bottom prices.

Her demeanor puzzled me, however. A distinct change seemed to be in the offing. Instead of oozing scorn, she dripped charm.

"May I come in?" she simpered, flashing her teeth at me. "I have a proposition to make to you."

Somewhat astonished, I opened the door and stood aside. Gladys made a beeline for Harry and proceeded very expertly to cajole him.

"Dear Mr. Holmes! I am in a terrible dilemma that I am hoping you, and", — here she paused and threw me a weak smile — "your good wife, will help with."

"Ooh you little cat," I thought. "What do you want now?" I smiled back at her.

Well, such a tale of woe she told us. It seemed the boarding house she ran on Cordova Street had just been sold from under her feet. As of the end of the month both she and her tenants would be homeless.

"There is nowhere for my tenants or myself to go. None of us has any family to take us in. I cannot afford to buy a place, so we will all be on the streets."

I was desperately trying to second-guess what she wanted. I had a horrid foreboding that it was going to affect us in some way, and I knew Harry's soft heart.

Sure enough, Harry was looking very sympathetic. Gladys took full advantage of this and, stepping up her tactics, gently laid her hand on his arm.

"Dear, dear Mr. Holmes, would you consider not selling this beautiful home, but renting it to me?" She dabbed sadly at the corner of her eyes with a tiny hankie.

The air was thick with the telegraphic message I was sending to Harry. "She's changed her tune. How dare she try and coax you with that trick of soulful tears? We're selling and getting out, aren't we?"

Harry patted her consolingly on the shoulders and told her he'd think it over. I could have screamed.

That night we sat with the Bostik family, trying to work out what to do. I was dead against any campaign aside from selling the house in order to retrieve our money and buy again in Edmonton.

Again Mr. Bostik gave us some sage advice. "I know you don't like this woman, Peggy, but listen to her plans carefully. They may be a viable alternative."

He was right. The housing market was so depressed we could be months trying to sell. If that happened we would miss the chance of Harry's returning to his old job and then we would really be sunk.

Gladys must have been listening to the conversation. Nine o'clock the next morning, she arrived on the doorstep with a big bunch of daffodils, plans of how to turn our house into apartments, and an impressive list of facts and figures. I knew we were lost as soon as Harry confessed he didn't know what to charge her for the rental.

After a long pause he hesitantly said, "How about ninety dollars a month?" We both looked at Gladys.

She laughed merrily. "But my dear Mr. Holmes, you won't even break even on that. I'll give you a hundred and twenty-five a month and bear the cost of converting the apartments."

We signed the lease the very next day. The date was April 1, and to this day I'm not sure who was the April fool.

From that moment Gladys adopted us. We had saved her and her lodgers from joining the many homeless Vancouverites, and she couldn't do enough for us. She even tolerated Bryan.

Thus, another exodus began.

Our furniture must have wondered what on earth we were up to. Some boxes had only just been unpacked when we began bundling things back into them in preparation for the return journey.

Mother took one look at the mess and decided to visit her friends again. We promised to let her know as soon as we had suitable accommodation in Edmonton and waved her off with a sigh of relief. We now had one less person to worry about.

Things seemed to be working out quite nicely. The Bostik family were ready to return to their farm in Alberta and made their plans so we could all leave at the same time.

They had bought a car while in Vancouver, an old Chevy they planned to drive back for use on the farm. I looked at it and hoped it would last the journey. I still remembered vividly those roads across the deserts and mountains in the States. I felt very smug that Harry had bought us train tickets. We were going to enjoy a relaxed journey through the Canadian Rockies.

Thanks to Gladys, who was a dynamo, the packing went smoothly. She had arrived unexpectedly one day to find me haphazardly throwing things in boxes.

"Now Mrs. Holmes," she remonstrated, taking the curtains I

124

was folding. "That's no way to pack. Those lovely curtains will look like dishrags by the time you get to Edmonton."

Well I knew that, but if the alternative to stuffing everything in a box was me looking like a dishrag, then it was going to be the curtains.

Gladys watched for a while and I believe she thought we would never be out of the house. So she took over and labelled, packed and sorted. I have never been so organized before or since. There was a niggling doubt in my mind that things were going a little too smoothly, but I squelched it quickly before it could take root.

Fate agreed with me, and decided to liven things up. The day before we were due to depart, Mr. Bostik fell down the stairs and wrenched his right arm so badly it had to be strapped up.

This was a disaster. Mrs. Bostik had never driven a car and they didn't have the money to take the car and themselves on the train.

We had no alternative but to offer to drive the car back for them. They had been so very helpful to us, we could not leave them in the lurch.

Harry and I went out to look critically at the old Chevy. It seemed very small for two families, so Harry suggested Mr. Bostik try to pick up a trailer in which to pack the baggage, giving us all a bit more room.

A shaky little trailer was found and attached, but neither car nor trailer looked sturdy enough for the arduous trip ahead. There was nothing we could do about that. We just had to get on with it and hope for the best.

I did balk at putting my little chest of sterling silver in the trailer; I wanted it safely with us in the car. After all, it was the only valuable item we possessed. Harry persuaded me to put it in the back with the rest of the household effects, and not be silly.

Zero hour came and Gladys and her lodgers waved us off and wished us well. At the last minute she gave me a big hug, and thrust a forgotten toothbrush into my hand.

I returned her hug and genuinely wished her luck, and she stood waving, over the black stumps of the Douglas firs, until we were out of sight. I had no regrets in leaving that fifteen-room

headache. I just wondered how she was going to feed the furnace
now that the trees were gone.

26
Nightmare Ride

The roads were every bit as bad as I had remembered. The little
Chevy shivered and shook as it lurched from mud hole to boulder
and back. I clutched the side tightly, closed my eyes and tried not
to worry about how long it was going to take us to reach friendly
Alberta.

We stopped for a quick sandwich a couple of hours out of
Vancouver, and Harry and Mr. Bostik had a serious look at the
tires. They decided the remaining rubber was worn so thin, and
the roads were so bad, that the tires would not survive the trip
back to Alberta.

This was a fine old time to come to that kind of decision. We
were already in an isolated area and tires were not easily come by
even in Vancouver. The only thing to do was carry on and ask
about replacements along the way.

What a hope. It was the old old story: "Didn't you know there
was a war on?" There was not a tire to be had anywhere.

In the next four hours we had thirteen punctures.

To add to our problems Harry was not very well. He had
started with stomach cramps about an hour after eating his
sandwiches. As the day wore on he became progressively worse,
and we had to make increasingly frequent stops to allow him to
retire to the bushes. At first we all tried to laugh it off. But Harry's
face looked more pinched and drawn with each stop, and we
realized he was feeling very ill indeed.

We also detoured into every little settlement and scavenged in
its dump hoping to find tires in better shape than the ones we had.

The frequent stops and the worsening roads made our progress slow to a snail's pace. The cramped conditions and the worry about Harry turned the situation into a nightmare; I hope I never experience its likes again.

At one point the car's gas line blocked and Mr. Bostik struggled to blow through it and suck up the gas — a long tiresome job, made more difficult with his arm strapped up. Harry, desperately ill with what we could only assume was food poisoning, retired to a nearby railway embankment. I was horrified to see a train coming, but by this time Harry was too ill to care about spectators.

The awful day wore on, and we were travelling so slowly I didn't think we would ever reach a place where we could stop for the night. Suddenly I let out a yell and we all jolted forward as Harry jammed on the brakes. I had turned 'round to check that my silver was all right, and found the trailer was missing.

We leaped out of the car and ran to the cliff edge, expecting to see our belonging smashed to smithereens below us. Not a thing was in sight. Our hearts sank. The trailer could be several miles back, and goodness only knew how we were going to locate it unless it was at the side of the road.

We were lucky. Mrs. Bostik spotted it not far down the road. It had slumped drunkenly into a culvert, and apart from a few scratches the dents seemed to be all in one place. We didn't dare open it to see if anything inside was smashed.

Finally, we arrived at a small hamlet that boasted a hotel and a couple of motels, but to our dismay everything had a No Vacancy sign. We were desperate for a night's lodging as Harry was in such a dreadful state. Thank goodness we eventually managed to convince the hotel manager of our plight.

Once he realized Harry was ill, the manager could not have shown us more kindness. He sat us down and tried to see how he could help. We were in a small mining community, and the mine manager, who resided in a room on the top floor, had driven into Vancouver for a couple of nights. We could have his room, but it would only sleep the two of us; there were no spare beds. The Bostiks would have to push chairs together in the lobby and sleep on those.

This was a far from ideal solution. The lobby was small and crowded and everyone going to the bar would have to pass through. I fully expected Harry to suggest that Mrs. Bostik and I share the bedroom and the men sleep in the lobby.

Harry kept silent, however, and rushed me off to the bedroom. Once there, I realized why he was so anxious. He was bleeding profusely, and desperately needed a bath and a change of clothes. I did wish there was a way we could get him medical attention, but like the tires it was not to be had for love or money.

A hot bath and a good night's rest did seem to help Harry and the next day he appeared game to travel on. In fact he seemed in slightly better shape than the Bostiks.

They'd pushed together two hard couches and managed to make a bed with blankets from the hotel. They had just dropped off to sleep when they were rudely awakened by the late shift of miners coming in off-duty. Mrs. Bostik said she didn't know who was more startled, the men for walking into a makeshift bed in the middle of the hotel lobby, or them waking up from a troubled sleep to find a dozen dirty faces peering down.

We limped along for several days with neither Harry nor the tires showing any signs of improvement. Luckily we found a small drug store in one town. The druggist gave Harry some medicine that did offer a little relief, and made him promise to see a doctor if things didn't clear up almost immediately. Some hope.

By now Mr. Bostik, realizing that there were no tires to be had, decided to try to sell the car. Then we could all use the money to carry on our journey by train.

The only snag was, no one wanted to buy the old car.

We had travelled as far as Cranbrook B.C., and it didn't look as though we could dare go much further. In a last-ditch effort to find either tires or a prospective customer, Harry and Mr. Bostik walked over to the local garage. As expected, the proprietor thought they were mad and had nothing to suggest.

Just as they were about to leave, a small man who had been standing by listening spoke up.

"Say, I've some tires back at my place."

Harry and Mr. Bostik couldn't believe their ears.

"Stay there, while I get my truck and drive you over. It's

twenty miles back."

Harry didn't know what to think, but decided it was worth taking a chance. The truck drew up and off they bowled in a cloud of dust.

They had rather an odd conversation in the truck. The driver tried very hard to find out if they were religious and what church they attended. Harry and Mr. Bostik were a bit evasive, not caring much for the personal questions.

"I've been saved, you know," the man confided. "Changed my whole life, it did."

Harry began to wonder if they were in the company of the local eccentric. It seemed a very long twenty miles.

Eventually they reached an isolated farm, and with a screech of brakes pulled up in the yard.

Sure enough there were four tires, in good condition and right for the Chevy. Unfortunately, they were on the farmer's own car.

The men laughed good-naturedly at the joke, while wishing the man in Hades.

"No, no. You don't understand," said the little man earnestly. "I'm going to give you those tires off my car."

To the utter amazement of Harry and Mr. Bostik he started loosening the nuts and bolts on the wheels.

"I've been a very wicked man in my life."

Thunk! One tire was tossed in the back of the truck.

Harry tried to stop him and Mr. Bostik tried to pay him, but they were waved aside.

Thunk! Thunk! Two more tires landed in the back of the truck.

"Doing good deeds is my only hope of earning salvation, and this" he tossed the last tire up into the truck — "is one of them."

It was a very quiet journey back. Harry and Mr. Bostik were both moved and embarrassed by this gesture of help, but the small man happily whistled hymns as he drove along and refused to discuss the subject any further.

He helped us transfer the new tires onto our car and we gave him the old ones for whatever use he could make of them. Then we drove out of Cranbrook with his blessing.

As far as we were concerned that man deserved his salvation. For us he had performed a miracle.

27
The Return

How happy we were to see good old Edmonton once more. As we drove up the hill to the downtown area I felt as though we had never been away. It was good to see the familiar sights again and know we would fit right in.

Appearances can be deceiving, and during our six-month absence Edmonton had become a changed city. The Americans had arrived and Edmonton was a city under occupation.

Every hotel, motel and private room seemed to be occupied by enormous Texans. We had an awful job trying to find a room for the night, and eventually gave up and threw ourselves on the mercy of our long-suffering friends.

I had never imagined that having left Edmonton it might be difficult to pick up again. I assumed it would just be a question of finding a house and moving in.

No such luck. In our absence the Alaska Highway had been started.

The great influx of American workmen had totally changed Edmonton. They worked hard, drank hard, and really hustled to get things done in a hurry. As the highway was going to be a long job the Americans moved up here with their families and possessions. Everything was being done to make them feel at home. It has been said that the sign posts were altered to read south instead of north in order to keep the southerners on the job.

At the same time, secret deals were being negotiated between the United States and Russia, and Canada was involved. Washington was selling bombers to Moscow and flying them into Edmonton. Russian planes also flew in and unloaded strapping women pilots who then flew the bombers on to Russia. It's amazing that everyone in Edmonton knew what was happening, yet the rest of the world never caught on.

The tiny municipal airport had never seen such activity. Americans soon realized our concrete runways couldn't stand up to their heavy bombers, so they reinforced them for us. No expense was spared. It has always astonished me that no matter how deep the economic depression, as soon as war is declared money flies like popcorn for weapons and related equipment.

Construction was going on at such speed, you could watch the highway grow day by day.

An American foreman was bullying one of his compatriots to "get a move on and work a little faster."

"Heck," replied the man in a deep southern drawl, "Rome wasn't built in a day."

"Well I know nothing about that," said the foreman. "I wasn't on that job."

The stories about the Americans here were amusing but the situation wasn't so amusing to us. We were in another predicament. We needed a home.

Thank goodness Mother was safely visiting her friends at the coast. We sent Bryan, much to his delight, to stay at the Kirkwood dairy farm on the outskirts of Edmonton. There he could run wild to his heart's content while we combed Edmonton for another domicile.

Harry returned to the courts. After our horrendous trip home he was thirty-six pounds lighter but he seemed to have recovered fully.

With Harry away all day, I was the obvious person to do all the house hunting. It didn't matter where I looked, there was not a place to be had.

I was getting quite desperate when a friend, Dr. Harold Field, told me that a wonderful mansion, the Magrath Mansion, had been taken over by the city. The only occupant was a caretaker.

The Magrath Mansion was one of the wonders of early Edmonton. Built in 1912, it perched high on the riverbank at Ada Boulevard, lord of all it surveyed. William Magrath was an early real estate entrepreneur who developed the Highlands district, then fell into bankruptcy in the dirty thirties. His home was the second-biggest in Edmonton, only beaten by a short head by the Lieutenant-Governor's residence at the other end of the city.

Indeed this proud mansion remains one of the sights of

Edmonton, though it is not open to the public. It is now the residence and headquarters of the Ukrainian Catholic bishop.

During the war, however, it stood empty. This seemed wrong when there were people like ourselves struggling to find a place to live. With a picture in my mind of my favorite detective, Sherlock Holmes, I was off — hot on the scent!

This first clue led me to the city architect. I wheedled and needled him until he admitted that "yes, the city did own the Magrath Mansion and it would be perfectly possible to turn the ballroom on the top floor into apartments."

I was thrilled when he said he might even have a go at drawing up some plans, but he did give me a warning: "You will have to sell the idea to the City Commissioner, and I doubt he will go for it."

The next morning, off I went to try for an appointment with the City Commissioner.

The man did not waste any time. He looked at me briefly and in a businesslike manner asked, "Well, what do you want?"

As soon as I began talking about not having a place to live, he started pacing up and down his office like a caged lion.

"Everyone is on my back for accommodation," he accused. "There is just nothing I can do for you."

I started to tell him about my idea for the conversion of the Magrath Mansion, but he would not let me finish.

By this time I had had it. I sat down and did the only thing I could do in my situation. I sobbed.

This disconcerted him and he came over and begged me not to cry.

As I mopped my eyes I told him that the architect had drawn up some plans. The project was feasible, and the ballroom could be converted very easily. The commissioner was taken by surprise but after some thought, he said, tiredly, "Tell him to go ahead."

In a very short while we received the message: "You can move in."

The Magrath Mansion was set in a ten-acre estate, and we looked out on a pastoral scene across the river, where the country rolled away serenely into the distance. Now that beautiful country is covered with gas processing plants and known to all and sundry as Refinery Row. Progress has certainly changed the scene.

The apartment on the top floor of the mansion was to be only temporary and had not been fixed up with a proper kitchen. I had to use the marble bathroom to wash the dishes.

Living in that beautiful mansion I felt like Cinderella. My dream world was quickly shattered, however, when Mother arrived. She took one look at the gracious staircase and told us she couldn't possibly mount those every day. Besides ...

"Where's the bus stop?"

There wasn't one for a couple of miles.

"Where's the nearest store?"

At the bus stop.

I began to see that we had problems, and this wonderful place was not for us.

We sent out scouts, and eventually, while I enjoyed the mansion and Mother grumbled about it, we heard on the grapevine that there was a vacant house down by the Low Level Bridge, on the riverbank. It was a small modern bungalow situated, wouldn't you know it, directly opposite the concrete castle we had lived in on the Ross flats.

I felt sad leaving the Magrath Mansion, but grateful that we had found a house in which the family could be united.

And so I began another phase of my turbulent life.

28
War Efforts

Settling into a new home is always an adventure, and gradually my life began to take shape again. I stuck to my resolve to avoid frivolous coffee parties. Besides, the war was making demands on everyone. How could I stay uninvolved?

So many men were called into the services that, once again, women had to come out of the kitchen and learn some trades. Personally, I had never really been stuck in a kitchen, but I was eager to join the work force once more.

My friend, Dr. Harold Field, told me his office was in a dreadful state. His partner had enlisted, and Dr. Field was seeing a double load of patients.

To add to his troubles he had only one nurse, and with so many nurses joining the forces, he couldn't find another one.

He'd discussed the matter with his wife, Vi, and they'd decided to approach me to see if I was willing to work as a receptionist in his office.

I had already been a milliner, a banker, a homesteader and a plumber, so why not? This would be a new experience.

I arrived at the office wearing a white uniform and looking as professional as I could. I marched across the already packed waiting room and deposited myself firmly at the desk in the corner, feeling very important. All eyes swivelled around and fixed themselves on me.

Now what?

Determined to look as though I knew exactly what I was doing, I picked up a magazine from the desktop and flicked through it. This move would have been more impressive if I had held it the right way up.

Realizing my mistake I quickly tried to cram the magazine into the desk drawer. The drawers were locked. The eyes watched to see what I would do next.

Thank goodness Dr. Field arrived to put me out of my misery.

Heaven only knows what silly thing I would have tried. I swept triumphantly into the office and came out with a bunch of keys and a pile of files which I banged purposefully on the desk, and I fixed the eyes with a firm glare.

"Who's first?" To my surprise there wasn't a concerted rush. And so my new career began.

Every day for the first week a little birdlike woman would turn up first thing in the afternoon. I would present her file to Dr. Field but he always waved it away, saying, "Hmm, yes, well I'll see the next patient and you can send her in later."

Several patients later, I would present her file again and the same routine would take place.

Miss Allison, the patient, would sit motionless with a faraway look in her eyes and a smile on her face.

I thought this was a very odd situation. I had known Dr. Field for years and had never thought he was the sort of person to ignore a patient.

I would jog his memory several times, but each time I got the same answer: "Later."

Eventually, just before he was due to close his office, Dr. Field would come out and beckon to Miss Allison. Then, in less than two minutes, she would scuttle out of the office with a big beam across her face.

Dr. Field would come out mopping his brow.

"What on earth was all that about?" I asked at last.

Dr. Field sheepishly explained that there was nothing at all wrong with the woman's health; she just had a bruised heart. I looked concerned and then realized he meant Miss Allison had a crush on him. Poor man. I was able to fend her off several times after that week.

All was not smooth sailing in the doctor's office. One day a very suspicious patient suddenly leaned over the desk and said, "You're new. Where did you graduate?"

I drew myself up to my full height and said, firmly, "England" — while quaking in my boots.

Thank goodness she didn't pursue my qualifications further and ask what hospital.

Despite my inexperience I did manage to keep my common

sense firmly in place. I managed also to keep my sense of humour. Both served me well, for a doctor's office is certainly the sort of place where anything can happen.

One day a young office boy dashed in and slapped a twenty-six ounce bottle of liquid on my desk.

"Mom's sent a sample," he grinned, and dashed out again.

My most embarrassing moment occurred when the professional nurse had her day off and a patient came in with some cracked ribs. The doctor needed to strap up his ribs but, as the patient was a very large and hairy man, asked the substitute nurse to shave him first.

I don't think Dr. Field realized what he was asking.

The substitute nurse tried her best, but making no headway came and asked me to help her.

I looked at the razor and thanked my stars it was one of the safety type. Even so the edges of the blade seemed to gleam wickedly and my hand shook.

Approaching the patient with a cheery smile to distract him from our shaking hands, we attacked on both sides and planned to meet around his navel. It was a hopeless task — something like trying to attack a fur rug with nail scissors — and the poor man gave a yelp of agony.

Cheerfully we smiled and joked, hoping to distract him, but we were obviously getting nowhere. The razors clogged every few minutes.

The nurse decided another approach was needed. She asked the patient to bend over so we could try to shave his back. The man co-operated and we gazed at the resulting expanse with dismay; it was hairier than his front. I launched my attack by trying to cut a swath across the middle while the nurse tried to meet me from her side.

This was even more hopeless. The man not only was hairy, he was ticklish. Every time we touched him under the arms he had to stifle his giggles. The razor got stuck regularly and we began to have trouble keeping our own faces straight. A suppressed snort from the victim did it. We all succumbed to gales of laughter that brought Dr. Field rushing in.

We were so convulsed with laughter that we couldn't explain a thing to the doctor, but just waved the razors helplessly in the air. The patient took pity on us.

"Ooh," he said. "Your nurses are tickling me to death, and I haven't laughed so much since my wife died."

Dr. Field looked at us, raised his eyebrows and gently suggested that as it was six o'clock, perhaps we would like to go off duty. He would finish the job.

It was not long after this episode that Dr. Field made a determined effort and managed to find a real nurse to help him out.

Just before my last day, the doctor's wife, Vi Field, asked me if I would be interested in a secretarial job at the Woman's Volunteer Bureau. The Northwestern Utilities Company had donated a desk and some office space in their building, and the bureau now needed someone with experience to help establish the office. This was something I could do well. I started work with the head of the bureau, Mrs. Arnold Taylor, and we worked together for several years.

In a job such as this one you make many contacts, and it wasn't long before I found myself serving on the board of the Red Cross Society along with Vi Field.

The war news was ghastly and we all wanted to do something to help our homeland, so Vi headed up a committee to meet the army personnel trains coming into the Canadian National and Canadian Pacific stations.

Vi called several of the Red Cross women into action. We all worked in offices near the stations, so we managed to slip out when the trains were in.

As soon as the call came that a troop train was due, I would grab my basket of magazines, cigarettes and chocolates and dash down to the station to meet up with the Canadian Legion workers and the YWCA Travellers' Aid helpers.

At this time, British and Canadian forces were being moved across from the east coast to the west coast. I remember asking one young sailor what he thought of the prairies.

"I've never seen so many bloody miles of nothing in all my life."

After the movement of forces, trains carrying war brides

137

began to trickle through. Some of the brides were here to join their wounded husbands. Others were coming to Canada to escape the bombings.

Some of our Red Cross girls had been sent over to England to escort them to Canada, but despite the help and support we provided, the war brides found life over here very strange and it took a while for them to adjust.

Soon the numbers of trains began to swell and the loads became much heavier. So we could greet as many travellers as possible, the Red Cross gave us a little cart we could wheel down the platform. As the young brides and mothers poured in we needed all the help we could get from the many organizations in town. Often the husbands were not there to meet them and the girls needed comfort and lodgings.

One starry-eyed girl called herself a princess. She knew her husband's father was a chief on an Indian reserve.

Now, forty years later, I am again meeting many of those war brides. We have formed a War Brides' Association, of which I am an honorary member. It is heartwarming to see how so many of them adjusted and became true Canadians.

The CNR stationmaster, Mr. Buckingham, was a splendid man. He took a personal interest in many of the travellers who disembarked at his station, and he tried to be helpful in the many problems we all were dealing with.

One young veteran, returning from service, arrived in an awful flap. He had been sorting out his things on the train and had lost a paper bag containing his money and papers. It had been accidentally thrown out the window with some rubbish.

Fortunately he remembered approximately how far back this had happened. Buck, as the stationmaster was affectionately called, ordered a handcar for the search. Not long afterward came a resounding cheer from the troops in the station. The soldier had arrived back, all smiles, with his money and papers safely recovered.

One night we were alerted that a special trainload of British soldiers who had been prisoners of war in Hong Kong was due to come through Edmonton.

One of our group had a brainwave. We would put up signs all

along the platform giving the names of towns and cities in England that we had contact with. Anyone from one of these places would gather under its sign to meet and exchange news about the people they knew.

Harry and I stood under Hull, England. A few people gathered around us and among them Harry discovered a cousin who we thought had been killed long ago. This sort of incredible coincidence happened to many people during the war.

All around us the most touching and pathetic scenes were being enacted. Many of the men were in a dreadful state physically, and often the relief of hearing news of their family and friends broke them down completely.

Some men were so ill they could not leave the train, and others were lifted out of the windows on stretchers. It was a heartbreaking sight.

The situation was not without amusing incidents, either. One little cockney lad strode around the platform proudly displaying a Japanese war sword nearly as big as himself. He told us that while in the camp a Japanese soldier had threatened him several times a day with that sword by brandishing it over his head. His one ambition through his internment was to capture that sword, and upon release he had dashed at the surprised soldier and grabbed the weapon. No one was going to part him from his souvenir.

Many stories were told that night of the hardships and the personal triumphs of the war. One soldier had been caught stealing food from the camp kitchens. The prison guards stood him out in the blazing sun, tied him up with his arms outstretched, and stuck a daikon in his mouth. Now a daikon is a kind of giant radish, and this specimen was about a foot long and as fat as a cucumber. Even though he was watched, the daikon disappeared. The guards were mystified and looked high and low for it. The prisoner had eaten it. Right down to the last mouthful.

29
Giving A Leg Up

May 8, 1945. Harry and I sat quietly at home with a couple of friends and celebrated Victory in Europe (V-E) Day. It was a curiously subdued celebration, not a bit like the emotional announcement at the end of the first world war.

That announcement had come on November 11, 1918, my twenty-first birthday. It was a miserable day; we were travelling by train to Southampton, where Harry was due to board a ship and return to the trenches in France.

The train drew into Grantham station and we were ecstatic to hear all the bells ringing, and the news of the armistice on everyone's lips. We fell on our knees in tears in the middle of the railway carriage, and thanked God the war was over and Harry would never have to fight again. In those naive days we all thought the War to End All Wars had been fought and true peace was ahead.

By 1945 we were all sobered by the fact there was no end to man's inhumanity. Of course Victory in Europe was not the true end to the war. Fighting still raged over the Pacific, and many of our friends and relatives were either involved in combat or interned in Japanese prison camps.

I will never forget the horror we felt when the news of the atomic bombs exploding over Hiroshima and Nagasaki came over the airwaves. I couldn't believe such dreadful weapons had been used. It made us feel that nothing would ever be the same again. We were right.

This sense of horror totally clouded Harry's and my celebration at that final end of the war, and again we sat quietly at home while the rest of Edmonton went wild.

Victory in Japan (V-J) Day was eventually celebrated on August 15, 1945, and strait-laced Edmonton became unrecognizable. When the city finally decided to let its hair down, it did so flamboyantly. Flags, fireworks, music and dancing were the

140

order of the day. Strangers linked arms and paraded down Jasper Avenue singing Keep the Home Fires Burning and other patriotic war songs.

Stores along Jasper Avenue presented special displays. The Johnstone Walker department store display sticks in memory; their window was adorned by two garbage cans, one filled with swastikas, the other with Rising Sun flags. Above them hung the cryptic message: That's That!

Unfortunately, the effects of the war were not dealt with quite as easily. Listening to the victors claiming zones in Berlin made me wonder if war was about to break out again. They were certainly sowing the seeds of future strife.

Edmonton itself was going through a great deal of change. The Alaska Highway was complete, but many of the Americans had married Edmonton girls and stayed in Canada. Our men were trickling back from the war and many of them brought sweethearts and wives from overseas. The women here, who had found freedom from housework, were reluctant to give up their good jobs, and the Turner Valley oil field seemed to be running dry. The outlook was black. Had we finished with the turmoil of war only to enter another depression?

Nothing but doom and gloom was predicted by the economists.

I never had time to worry. Upon the disbanding of the Woman's Volunteer Bureau, I was immediately requested to help form the Edmonton board of the Cancer Society.

After watching a friend battle with this dreadful disease I was only too willing to assist, and we decided to start a campaign raising money to help families cope with terminal cancer patients who left hospital to be nursed at home.

First we had to have an office. The Hudson's Bay Company came up trumps and we established our headquarters in their downtown Jasper Avenue store. The Alberta Travellers' Association also helped with funding, and we got ready to launch our campaign.

All seemed to be going smoothly and many eminent Edmonton women volunteered their services, including Mrs. Clarke, the wife of the mayor, after whom Clarke Stadium is named.

We sat around the boardroom table in a very businesslike fashion and mapped out a campaign that looked both impressive and workable. Then we realized that we needed an official board of directors and a president. Well, the board was no trouble at all; we were all there and all willing to stand. The problem was the president. In order to be taken seriously, we had to have a man.

This seems laughable now, but in the late forties it was no laughing matter. After much thought I suggested Ronald Martland, the son of the man who had designed our apartment in the Magrath Mansion. He was an important lawyer here in town, just the person we needed to give credibility to our operation.

We really had to twist his arm to make Ronald accept. I carefully explained that all we needed was his name; all the board members and other women volunteers would do the canvassing. What suckers we women were then.

Despite the odd setback, our first campaign was a resounding success.

Ronald Martland eventually left Edmonton to take up a federal position in Ottawa, eventually becoming Chief Justice of Canada, and with the loss of our token man I had to look for another president. I turned my sights toward G.R.A. Rice. Dr. Rice, as he is now, was the owner of CFRN Sunwapta Broadcasting, one of the first radio stations in Alberta. He made us an excellent president for many years.

I did not spend all my years with the society choosing their presidents. We all took turns making house calls to the stricken families.

One day I was instructed by the society to call at an address in east Edmonton. A friend offered to go with me, and we found an older couple in a nice little house complete with a canary chirping away in the corner of the living room.

The man, who was the patient, seemed fairly comfortable, but it was his wife who upset me. Her leg had been recently amputated at the knee, and she was in great distress because she could not afford an artificial limb.

Because she was not a cancer patient I knew our society could not help her, but I felt someone must. I decided to take matters into my own hands and resolved to approach the city Health and

Welfare Department and see if I could persuade them literally to give her a "leg up."

That stirred up a hornet's nest. The city couldn't go around giving out legs to everyone, could they? Besides, who was going to pay for it?

I suggested the city officials phone the Government of Alberta's Health Department, and after a series of discussions, with even more lobbying from me, the powers that be decided the city and the province would share the expense.

I breathed a sigh of relief, which was cut short when the city official turned to me and said, "Of course, you will have to be the one to transport her for her fittings."

My heart sank. I had a tiny car and the patient was a very large woman. How on earth was I going to haul her in and out? Luckily a sister society member came to the rescue, and between us we managed to ferry the woman to and fro. After numerous fittings, the woman was able to walk on her new appendage.

This dear soul referred to us as angels and invited us to a turkey dinner at her house. She happily told me she had some lovely plump ones in her deep freeze.

I couldn't believe my ears. I had been driving all over town asking officials for a free leg and things for a woman who could afford a deep freeze. Neither my friend nor I could afford that.

I ruefully related this story to one of the city's health officials, who burst out laughing. "Oh Peggy," he spluttered. "You conned us into supplying a leg for that lovely couple. They weren't even married."

Imagine my embarrassment. I'd signed endless papers for that couple and apparently perjured myself left and right. According to the morals of those days, they were living in sin. Still, even sinners need a leg up.

Not long after this incident, my duties took me to an old man in the General Hospital. This dear old chap cried and cried and told me he hadn't eaten any solid food for months, not because of illness but because he had no teeth.

Again my sympathies were aroused and off I went to City Hall. The health official saw me coming and clutched his forehead. "What do you want this time?" he cried.

143

"Teeth," I replied, and related the old man's sad story. Sure enough I managed to touch the heart of the bureaucracy and wheedled a set of choppers for him. A few weeks later I popped in to see my old patient and was delighted to find him tucking into a hearty meal. Sad to say, that was his last one. He died during the night.

I never felt my efforts on his behalf had been in vain, for who wants to die without teeth? Besides, the condemned man had really enjoyed his last supper.

I met the same official one more time. An elderly lady had confided to me that she was so hard up she was contemplating suicide. She didn't even have a loaf of bread in the house.

She was quite a lady and I was very sorry to see her in such straitened circumstances.

Once again I pleaded my case to this helpful official, and he said he would give me a cheque for a bag of groceries. He was munching on a tablet from a bottle of vitamins while we conversed, so I suggested he throw in a few pills for the poor woman. Happy to get rid of me so easily, he pushed the bottle toward me, saying, "Here, take the lot."

Needless to say, I did.

30
A Case Of Forgery

For years I had been using the mail to defraud. I had written letters signed with a name not my own. Now, it seemed, I was about to pay the penalty.

It all started when Harry, as a young man, enlisted in the 31st Battalion in Calgary way back in 1914. He made friends with a young Scot, Wee Jimmy Smith. Miraculously both Wee Jimmy and Harry came through the war relatively unscathed, and they

Some of the pupils at the Lynwood Kindergarten. Bryan is second from the left.

Peggy's mother, Rose Lewis, in 1939. She always loved her fur wraps.

Photo: Historic Sites, Alberta

The historic Magrath Mansion, where Peggy washed the dishes in a marble bathroom.

The car crash in 1958, one of the series of nasty incidents that happened around the 25th of the month the year after the mysterious ball of light on Christmas Eve.

Peggy, at age 73, selling her paintings at a local flea market.

Peggy and Harry in 1976. This photo was taken just before Harry's death.

Peggy receiving the Alberta Achievement Award in 1977 from Peter Lougheed, Premier of Alberta.

Peggy, Canada's oldest broadcaster, on CBC's Early Morning Show with Larry Langley.

made great plans for all they were going to accomplish when they returned to Canada.

Unfortunately Wee Jimmy's father died at the end of the war, leaving Jimmy a fishing trawler and a plea to "take care of Mother." Reluctantly, Jimmy headed back to Fifeshire and became a fisherman.

We lost contact with him for several years, but one day a friend who had been visiting the old country told us that he had seen Wee Jimmy. Jimmy was still fishing, but talked constantly of his old army buddies and especially Harry. Could Harry write to him?

Harry was so busy with his court transcripts that he had no time to write to anyone. In fact, I handled all our family correspondence. My heart was touched, however. I would write to Wee Jimmy and let him think that the letters were coming from Harry.

I started by reminiscing about their times together in the trenches. Heavens, I had heard those old stories so many times I could recite them by heart. Jimmy wrote back almost by return post. His letter was full of joy that Harry had remembered him and written. Good. We were off to a great start.

The correspondence continued for many years. Sometimes I had to check details with Harry for names, dates and places, and I always read him Jimmy's letters and my replies.

These letters from a so-called uneducated fisherman are some of my most precious possessions. Wee Jimmy spent many hours out on his boat with only the sea for company. His thoughts could take wing and he had a great gift for poetry. Every letter he wrote was worthy of publication. They were interesting, well written and incredibly beautiful.

It never occurred to me that I was being dishonest. The joy my letters so obviously gave Wee Jimmy made everything worthwhile. Besides, I thought, I would never meet him.

I was dead wrong.

The year after the second world war, Harry and I decided to take a trip to England. This would mean leaving Bryan behind with Mother — we didn't want to disrupt his schooling — but we needed to reassure ourselves that our family and friends had survived the war and were coping with the hardships of rationing that was still in force.

We received an invitation to go to Scotland, and Harry was delighted. He insisted we put Edinburgh on our itinerary and meet up with Wee Jimmy.

We arrived in England with mixed emotions. We were so happy to see our families again, but the devastation to places we knew was a shock.

Everywhere, great holes gaped at us: mementos left by Mr. Hitler's bombs that would take years to rebuild. There was a terrible beauty associated with these bomb craters. Wild forget-me-nots and fireweed grew in vivid blue and pink carpets over the debris — bright patches of color appearing unexpectedly in the heart of the cities.

England was nearly on its knees. The after-effects of the war were almost as deadly as the war itself. So many didn't come home. Those who did often had uncertain physical and mental health. Not one family we knew had been left unscathed.

Hundreds of the demobbed soldiers could not find work; fine repayment for men who had fought to save their country. It was sad to see them walking the streets desperately looking for work. Especially sad were the young men, many still in their mid-teens, who'd been forcibly plunged into a horrible adult world of bloodshed and killing and were not trained to do any other job. With no place in a peaceful world for these young people, it was no wonder the British morale was incredibly low.

Life, however, was not without its funny side. Visiting my cousin in Hull, we were startled to find her standing by the kitchen sink with her gas mask on. Once I'd recovered from the shock she gave me — she looked like an alien from outer space — I plucked up courage to ask why she was wearing it.

"Well, it didn't do me a ha' porth of good during the war, but I keeps it in the china cabinet and uses it when I peels onions."

When we'd first heard that tea was being rationed in England, I'd sent this cousin a bunch of tea bags. I should have saved the postage. Later in the visit she flabbergasted me by remarking, "By the way, that's funny lavender you have in Canada. It don't smell very nice."

She had been putting the tea bags in amongst her underwear.

Some aspects of Britain never change. In order to squeeze the most out of our visit, Harry and I decided to use our gas coupons and hire a little Morris Minor. Then, in true North American fashion, off we went to see the country and call on some of our friends. We horrified most of them with the amount of travelling we did. One friend told us that he wouldn't consider going forty miles for less than a week's holiday. Venturing up and down the country with a day here and there was something only madmen and Americans undertook. We didn't dare tell them about our trips through the mountains.

I'd always loved the tiny country villages and it was a great relief to find that the war had left great chunks of English countryside still intact, though poor, hungry and short of luxuries.

Passing through a picturesque village in Sussex, we started to look for somewhere to eat lunch. In the market square our eyes lit upon a beautiful Georgian house. On the door was a neat sign, "Rosemary's Studio — Meals."

Upon ringing an elegant brass doorbell, we were ushered into a large hall. This was quite obviously someone's home. Personal touches were everywhere. Fresh flowers graced well-polished surfaces, and framed photos of various members of the family hung on every wall. We surmised that due to reduced circumstances the family had decided to serve meals to the gentry.

The dining room was beautiful. We sat at a table for two by the window, overlooking an old-fashioned walled garden with sundial, birdbath and lawns like green velvet.

At this point a gangling young girl loped over and, in a broad cockney accent, recited a piece to us, all in one breath. To our amazement we realized that she was reciting the menu. After making her repeat this twice we remained bewildered and she was very breathless, so I latched onto the only word I had understood.

"Thank you, dear. We will have the fish."

It was like rubbing Aladdin's lamp. She re-appeared beaming, and firmly plonked two portions of flaccid-looking fish on our plates. The fish didn't look as though this kind of brisk treatment had done it any good, but the setting we were in more than compensated for the food.

Harry and I felt as though we had stepped into a movie on English country life. In fact, J. Arthur Rank couldn't have peopled that house more vividly than the characters who were sitting around us.

At the next table was the village parson, so typical it was laughable. He even looked like Alec Guinness. Three county types were sitting at another table. They were loudly discussing the mortgages on the old family home and the appalling taxes and death duties. The lady in this trio had taken elocution lessons and wanted everyone to know. I suppressed a terrific urge to lean over and give some good Canadian advice such as, "Go to your local credit union."

The village schoolmaster was chatting earnestly in the corner and I had just leaned over to Harry to whisper, "Isn't this wonderful, it has everything you could ask for," when in walked two dashing men from India, in full national dress.

Dessert time arrived, and with it our waitress. She dealt with the fishy remains in her usual express manner, and then began the second part of her recitations. This time the only word I recognized was plum duff, so we had that. It was mysterious but quite nice.

We came to the end of our meal and were about to depart when three more characters entered the dining room.

This party was dominated by an old, old man with a long, yellowish beard. He shuffled in, bending low over two sturdy sticks and supported on one side by a weary looking lady who I assumed was his daughter, and a weedy young man who looked like his grandson.

They sat at a nearby table and we immediately knew that the old man's infirmities included deafness. All three shouted a general conversation for a while and then, in a piercing whisper, the old man requested "a walk down the garden path." The young man didn't look too pleased, but he heaved the old man up and off they trundled through the French windows, following the discreet arrows painted on the crazy paving.

Later as I followed the arrows myself I found that the elegance

148

of the place did not extent to the outside amenities. The some-what primitive outhouses were back to back and I could hear the young man struggling with the old gent while trying to carry on a civilized conversation.

The young man was shrieking, "Aren't the wisterias beautiful this year?" After the third repetition the old man replied. "Yes, the aroma is overwhelming."

I was convulsed but managed to restrain myself until Harry and I were safely back in our car. Off we drove, on the wrong side of the road, ready for more adventures and colorful characters.

For me the trip around England couldn't last long enough. All too soon we were ready to take up our invitation to Scotland and Nemesis approached. I had to face Wee Jimmy.

Obviously, I had great misgivings about this meeting, espe-cially when Harry absentmindedly dropped out that Jimmy didn't like women. Apparently they made him feel shy and uncomfortable. I didn't dare reveal how I was beginning to feel.

We met Jimmy on Edinburgh's famous Princes Street. He was waiting by the Scott Monument, looking like any of the thou-sands of men who attend the Saturday afternoon football games. He was small, of grey complexion, and wore the inevitable cloth cap and overcoat.

Jimmy took one look at me and swept me aside as unimpor-tant. He had eyes only for Harry.

Quickly I arranged to go shopping and the men promised to meet me for lunch.

I don't know what they talked about that morning, but at lunchtime they were relaxed and happy. Jimmy took us to a very ordinary little café, where he was the perfect host. This was to be his day and he looked after our meal as though we were royalty. During the meal he gradually became aware of me as a person, and by dessert he was hesitantly calling me Peggy. He gave me to understand that English women were not too highly regarded in Scotland, but conceded that as I was a Canadian I'd "pass."

To my surprise Jimmy invited me to join them for the after-noon. He'd planned to show us the castle. With great pride he waved away the guide and began a personal tour. He knew every bit of its history.

The highlight came when he ushered us into the awe-inspiring memorial chapel. In one of my many letters to Jimmy I had told him that Harry's brother had been killed in France while in action with the Royal Scottish Regiment. Jimmy steered us toward the memorial book in the chapel. He had arranged for the name Charles Edward Grosvenor Holmes to be on display.

How touching it was to see tall Harry and Wee Jimmy standing side by side reading the epitaph to Harry's brother: "Killed in action — Armentières — World War One, 1918."

One of life's circles was complete; the two friends had met and there was no need ever to tell Jimmy I had written to him in lieu of Harry.

After this meeting in Edinburgh we corresponded for many more years, but now I'd won my spurs and gained a new friend. From now on the letters were always signed, Love, Peggy and Harry.

31
From The Ridiculous
To The Sublime

Like many other people, I was too busy living life to worry about middle age, but I suddenly became aware of a sag to my middle, a chin where never a chin used to be, and a distinct blurring of features. All this coincided with an advertisement for Streamline Parlours.

Streamline Parlours were the forerunners of the fitness centres we see today. The idea that beauty belongs to the masses and not just to the jet set was a new concept in the mid 1950s, and needing a morale booster, off I went.

It didn't take me long to realize that this might be a fly-by-night operation. Streamline pressured many customers into paying for lifetime memberships, and I was sure the company was not going to be around that long.

I'd been lucky enough to be in on a special deal, so I made the effort to attend every day in order to get my money's worth before Streamline disappeared.

I quite enjoyed pampering myself for a change. Our lives had been full of incident, but now for the first time in many years, I was finding a little spare time.

Bryan, by 1955, was a strapping young man who towered over me. Yes, despite my haphazard child-rearing, he'd survived and, at nineteen, had just married his high-school sweetheart.

Mother, still hale and hearty in her late seventies, was living with us. We had sold the store and were all glad to have that responsibility off our plate.

For once, there wasn't a cloud on our horizon and I had the time to take as many beauty classes as I liked.

Dashing out to my car in my usual rushed fashion, I was juggling letters to mail, my exercise clothing, my purse, and a couple of bags of garbage.

"Don't forget to pick up some bread," shouted my mother from the doorway. "And cash my pension cheque."

The garden was a blaze of color. I walked down the path admiring it, while adding the odd dead flowerhead to the garbage I was carrying.

The back lane garbage area was already overflowing. Our neighbor had pruned his trees and piled the branches high against the garage, leaving little room for me to open the garage door. I added my bags to the heap, glad that tomorrow was collection day.

Sitting in the sauna at Streamline, I experienced one of those horrid feelings that something was wrong. I replayed my actions since the time I had left the house, and suddenly I broke out in beads of perspiration that had nothing to do with the heat of the sauna. I clearly remembered mailing the letters on my way but, what on earth had I done with mother's pension cheque?

I had no recollection of a cheque being among my belongings when I mailed the letters, so there was only one possible place it

151

could be — I must have stuffed it in with the garbage.

Oh well, the garbage would still be there when I reached home. I settled down to sweat off a few more pounds, then made my way home via the Jubilee Auditorium. There I managed to pick up two last-minute tickets for the evening's performance of La Traviata.

Arriving home, I pulled into the back lane and gazed in horror at the spotless vista. Thank goodness the garbage truck was still in sight. I was only two houses away, and I could see the men industriously piling it high with other people's refuse.

I comforted myself with the fact that all was not lost, and tried not to think about how I was actually going to find the cheque in all the mess.

The driver and his mate were exceedingly helpful. They didn't speak English, but seemed to understand my frantic mime and the words "pension cheque." Climbing up on top of the debris, they poked around through my neighbor's branches and held up bag after bag of garbage.

All the garbage was in the same miserable state and it seemed impossible to identify my own sodden bags among the mess. I knew they would sink further into the mire the more the men trampled on the heaps, so finally I grasped the side of the truck and climbed up to join in. The men were delighted, and we all foraged through the branches and bags until, eureka, I actually recognized one.

Joyfully we upended it and there was the cheque, a little grimy and crushed but definitely redeemable.

The men and I spent some time slapping one another on the back and grinning. I was so impressed with their courtesy that I wrote a letter to the chief sanitary inspector. I felt someone should tell him about the high standard of cooperation among his employees.

Playing hunt the garbage bag made it imperative that I soak in the bath as soon as possible. What a difference hot water, well-seasoned with bath oil, makes. In no time I was ready to sally forth in evening dress and join my friend at the opera.

Sitting among the beautiful people, many of them in full evening dress, I thought what a strange day it had been.

The opera was drawing to its close with Violetta, the heroine about to die on the bed. As her lover clasped her in his arms and warbled his final aria lustily down her ear, the bed fell in.

We descended rapidly from grand opera to Italian farce as the principals disentangled themselves from the wreckage and tottered over to the window where Violetta could die less violently, in a convenient chair.

A couple of weeks later as I was backing my car out of the garage, I was stopped by the garbage truck. The men climbed out, bowed low and shook my hands. In broken English they told me that their manager had called them in, shown them my letter, and commended them for their work. Then as they drove off, I heard them singing Verdi.

Maybe that's the reason why every time I see a garbage truck I burst into snatches of La Traviata.

The middle years of my life continued to be as full of incident as the earlier years. I met many interesting people and participated in peculiar goings on. One of the strangest happenings occurred in 1957.

It was Christmas Eve and, true to our tradition, Harry and I were holding an open house for our friends. It was a cold, clear night, with no signs of a storm, and many guests dropped in to share our Christmas joy.

Toward midnight the crowd thinned out. Eventually there were just seven of us sitting comfortably in the living room. All was peaceful as we sat enjoying the flickering fire and colored lights on the Christmas tree.

Without warning, a vivid ball of blue light appeared at the top of the narrow window beside the fireplace, shot on a downward course in front of the tree, and disappeared through the floor. There was no sign of its entrance through the window, nor a mark left where it had grounded itself on the floor.

We gazed at the floor and at one another in utter astonishment, obviously relieved that we had all observed the same phenomenon. For a while no one moved; I think we all wondered if this was the start of some celestial bombardment or the Second Coming. Then we started to look for an explanation.

Everyone in the room, with the exception of my elderly mother who was chatting with a friend, had seen the blue blaze, and everyone offered his own interpretation.

On only two points were we all agreed: We hadn't imagined it, and because the tree lights were not affected, it was not a straightforward electrical fault.

One person suggested it was the exhaust from a passing car. We all ruled that out. Another thought it might have been from a lightning storm, but there was no storm. I had once read about St. Elmo's fire, a mysterious ball of light that gathered on the top of ships' masts. But heaven knows, we were far enough from the sea.

The memory of that strange ball of fire has never left me. It was not a welcome guest, and how terrifying it could have been to a young babysitter or an old person on their own.

Someone suggested it could be an omen but I quickly squashed that idea. Oddly enough, in the first few months of the following year our family suffered a series of accidents. Our car was wiped out in a freak accident on the Groat Road, I broke my arm, and my mother fell and injured her hip. All these things happened around the twenty-fifth of the month.

Strange, wasn't it?

32
Retirement

After forty-five years of pounding out evidence on his trusty typewriter, Harry decided to retire. For months he'd been plagued by eye trouble, and the specialist had come to the conclusion that he was suffering from a form of snow blindness caused by the many years of typing on white paper in glaring light.

He announced his decision quietly and was taken aback by the ensuing uproar in the courts. Anyone would think the judicial system couldn't survive without him. The furor left him unruffled. Harry firmly believed no one was indispensable and he was quite sure someone could step into his shoes.

Little did we know that Harry would retire three times.

Each time, he was called back to help with an emergency situation, and after the situation had been resolved everyone obviously hoped he would stay put.

We attended several farewell parties, and Harry was acknowledged as "the man of a billion words." He had written up more murders than any other reporter and was the court reporter for the last case in Alberta in which the accused received the death penalty by hanging.

Finally, at eighty years of age, Harry wrote his last case in the Supreme Court. Then, with yet another bang-up party, he finally departed with the good wishes of the Alberta judicial system ringing in his ears. We knew this definitely was the grande finale. By now, Harry's eyes were so bad he could never go back to work. In fact, he was registered with the Canadian National Institute for the Blind.

In recognition of his long years of dedicated service the courts left his name plate on his office door until the day the wrecker's ball demolished the beautiful old building to make room for the new Woodwards store.

We had no intention of retiring into oblivion. We were going to take advantage of every opportunity that came our way and enjoy ourselves.

Close on the heels of retirement came an invitation to stay in a mobile home in Burnaby, B.C. The owners were on a long trip around North America and wanted someone in their trailer for at least part of the time. I took charge, arranged for Mother to stay in a guest house for refined ladies, bundled Harry into the car, and off we set for a peaceful holiday away from it all.

I should have known better.

The name Coastal Vista Auto Court had really appealed to me, and I'd imagined a mountainside retreat overlooking the City of Vancouver. Reality was a little different. Sure you could see the occasional mountaintop — if you caught it early in the morning, when the smog, exhaust fumes and dust from the busy highway was at a low ebb. The rest of the time there were so many big trucks rattling past that you couldn't see a thing, or even make yourself heard over the roar of the traffic.

I remarked to Harry that the trailer court seemed to be in a sleazy neighborhood, but because he couldn't see it he wasn't too disturbed, and we settled in quite nicely.

Each morning I followed a routine of reading the top news stories to Harry. Coffee and interesting scandal are always a good way to approach the day. You can comment uninhibitedly around the kitchen table and, after setting the world to rights, embark confidently on your own business.

The main news story at that time was the escape of two murderers from the penitentiary not far away. They were being sought in the mountains around Burnaby and for ten days warranted front page attention. I would read the latest report to Harry and then put the paper to much better use. I needed it to waft about — it created an excellent draft — to get the stove to light each morning.

This stove was the bane of my existence. There were no instructions with it and no matter how I tried pushing levers, buttons, draught and doors, nothing made the darn thing function reliably.

After we'd settled in, I bought a turkey and invited friends from Vancouver to join us for dinner. That day I couldn't get the stove to work at all, no matter how hard I wafted.

By this time, I had met the people next door, a commune of young hippies who, despite their odd appearance, seemed friendly. I knocked tentatively on their door and asked if they had any idea how to make my stove work. One of the young men came over and took a look. He fiddled and poked and turned knobs, and the stove responded fitfully but not enough to cook my turkey.

Eventually I went to the trailer park office. The manager couldn't make the stove work either, but offered to pop the turkey in her oven and bring it over when it was done.

The bird arrived, done to a turn, just as my guests rang the doorbell. They wondered what on earth I had been up to with a

156

full-blown turkey arriving on the doorsteps in a wire basket. I smiled calmly and asked if they had heard of chicken on the go? They nodded. "Well, this is turkey on the go" I explained, with my tongue in my cheek.

Our party was a great success and the guests didn't leave until the early hours of the morning. I laughed as I waved them off. "Look," I cried, pointing to the darkened trailer next door. "They're supposed to be the hippies and we're the ones partying late."

Harry and I fell on our bed and were immediately asleep. Abruptly we were awakened by a terrific disturbance outside. I leapt up and peeped through the curtains.

Red lights were flashing and sirens howling, and the police were swarming all over the place. It was a terrible commotion. Our first thought was that one of the trailers was on fire, but there seemed to be no fire engines, just great numbers of police. Then the door of the trailer next to us opened, and out came the young people handcuffed to several officers.

"Oh well," I thought. "So that's a drug bust. What a pity; they seemed nice young people." And we went back to sleep.

Turning on the radio the next morning we were astounded to hear the top story of the day: Dangerous murderers arrested at Coastal Vista Trailer Court.

"No wonder he couldn't fix your stove," commented Harry.

A dignified friend in West Vancouver was horrified and phoned us up at once, instructing us to leave that awful place and stay with her. We did. Two days later a corpse was found in her apartment entrance.

Fortunately that seemed to be the end of the incidents, and for the rest of our visit we enjoyed a much needed quiet time. In fact life eventually became so quiet I decided we'd better come home.

No sooner the word than the deed. We threw everything in the car and left Vancouver late one afternoon, planning to make Hope by night. I like Hope; it is such a pretty little town, and I knew an excellent motel there.

Everything was running smoothly. I settled down to long-distance driving and began to make myself more comfortable by removing all unnecessary trimmings. Jewellery, scarf, sweater, earrings and, finally, my wig, were all tossed into Harry's lap. He never knew what I was going to hit him with next. Neither did I.

As we approached Agassiz there was a detour, and I was horrified to discover it was deep loose gravel. Then, unexpectedly, as I was ploughing through very carefully, we were propelled forward at a terrific rate. There was a loud crunch and the car stopped with Harry and me leaning forward, resting our heads on the dashboard. Nothing moved.

Without budging, I whispered, "Harry, are you all right?"

"I think so," he replied, also whispering. "But I think the car is in a lot of trouble."

And there we remained, too scared even to raise our heads and look at the damage.

A shadow moved to my side of the car. I turned my head to see a huge man looking in through the driver's window. He was obviously terrified, and he nearly passed out when we moved.

"God! I thought I'd killed you."

I turned around slowly to look at the back of our car and saw no back — just the front end of an enormous foodliner with a trailer.

"Goodness, I'm not surprised if you hit us with that. It's as big as a freight train."

We climbed out to survey the damage, and it seemed truly a miracle that we were alive. The foodliner had ploughed into our rear, and in its efforts to stop, the trailer had jackknifed across the road. Thank goodness we'd no back-seat passengers. The rear of our little car was a concertina.

Funnily enough our engine started. The truck driver appeared beside us. "Can I catch a ride with you? I can't move my lot."

Luckily I remembered there was a gas station not too far back, so this giant man squashed himself inside our car. Just then, another car drew up. A minister and his wife had seen our accident and offered to act as witnesses.

I decided I was all for religion.

I drove gingerly and eventually we all arrived at the gas station. Much to our relief there was not only a phone but also a motel. The Hope police came, and by the time the lengthy forms were filled in it was late and we were feeling tired and shaky.

The police were kind and assured us the accident was not our fault, but they needed me to go back with them to the scene of the crash.

Finding the place in the dark was not easy. Imagine my horror when the police said we were out of their territory and would have to call Agassiz and go through the whole rigmarole again.

It was long past midnight when we eventually got to bed.

When they checked our car in the morning the garage people found it looked a lot worse than it was. The back was all bent and the bumper and muffler missing, but the expert opinion was, "Drive slow and carefully, Ma'am, and you'll make it back to Edmonton. It'll just sound like hell."

They were right.

We drove into Hope and had a meal. Returning from the coffee shop we were surprised to find a paper cup, containing lovely red roses, balanced on our hood. That must be British Columbia, I figured. They bumped you at night and left red roses in the morning.

Harry thought someone had heard us limping in and, believing our car was in its death throes, sent a floral tribute.

Actually, in my heart of hearts I think our guardian angel was working overtime. Despite all odds we arrived home safely and managed to enjoy Harry's retirement for eight more good years.

Mother was quite elderly by now and, considering her age, hale and hearty. The demise of our car meant she needed a cab for her occasional trips. She was about to phone for a taxi one afternoon when the doorbell rang.

Opening the door I found two smartly dressed young salesmen who asked to speak with Mother. I showed them into the living room and told Mother that she had guests.

One of the young men raised his voice and bellowed, "I understand you are hard of hearing."

"Just a second, young man," replied my mother. "I want to turn off my hearing aid. You're deafening me."

Instead of taking the hint, the two men tried to talk my mother into buying some new and very expensive hearing equipment. I stayed around in case Mother couldn't deal with them, but I needn't have worried.

The salesman continued. "You could have a new hearing attachment built onto your glasses," he shouted.

"I only wear my glasses for reading," countered Mother. "What happens the rest of the time?"

The young man seemed a little puzzled.

"Besides," continued Mother, "how much does this new equipment cost?"

The young man brightened. "Only six hundred and ninety-five dollars, and if you give us the name of someone else you receive a ten dollar rebate."

Mother roared with laughter. "Nearly seven hundred dollars at my age. That would be silly, I'd never get my use out of it. Anyway I like the nice cheap one I'm already using."

Mother showed the young men to the door while still chuckling. Then she saw the fancy car waiting outside.

"Good heavens, is that your car?"

The young men nodded.

"If you are going toward the downtown area I'd be awfully happy if you'd offer me a lift."

I waved them off and awaited Mother's return with interest.

"What on earth did they say?" I asked as she came in the door.

"Nothing much," she replied. "But they took the MacDonald hill at an awful clip."

Unfortunately, Mother's health soon deteriorated. I found myself looking after her and steering Harry around and, being no spring chicken myself, became extremely tired. Eventually for all our sakes the doctors recommended that Mother go into a senior lodge. After several happy years there she moved again, this time to the Jubilee Nursing Home. Six months before she died she was so physically frail she was moved to the Allen Gray Hospital where at the age of 97 she peacefully passed away, her farewell remarks to us being, "Cheerio, take care of yourselves."

33
Stick 'Em Up

Thanks to our B.C. adventure, we needed a new car.

"Better make it a good one," remarked Harry. "Then it will see us out."

We looked at many makes and colors of cars, then someone told us of a new Datsun dealer in Calgary who was offering rock-bottom prices to attract customers.

Never being able to resist a bargain, off we went.

We were glad we made the trip. We found on sale a lovely little Datsun station wagon that was perfect for us, both in design and price. There was only one problem — it was an automatic.

The salesman was surprised when I asked how an automatic worked. I'd been taught in the days of stick shifts, I explained, and I wasn't at all sure that an automatic car was a good idea.

In order to calm my fears he took us to the Stampede Grounds, where I could drive around safely and experiment without causing a major traffic holdup or accident.

It was a beautiful day. We peacefully circled the grounds while the salesman patiently explained the car to me. When I felt confident, I took over and off we went again.

Passing the horse barn for the second time, Harry, who had been sitting silently in the back seat, suddenly piped up, "That's where that fellow shot me."

I was concentrating on the car, so I just grunted in reply. The salesman obviously thought Harry was a bit crackers.

Passing the barn on yet another circuit, I turned my head and looked at it. "Oh, he shot you in front of the horse barn?"

The salesman looked at us in horror and I could read his mind perfectly: "Heavens. Two loonies."

I drove around the grounds again and eventually pulled up beside the barn. I felt it was time to explain our startling remarks to the baffled salesman.

It was a story that went back to the first world war. In 1914, as

161

soon as war was declared, Harry and his mates had rushed down to Calgary to enlist in the 31st Battalion, which was assigned the horse barn as a training area.

One day, while they were standing around outside, one of the soldiers demonstrated the revolver he'd recently been issued.

"Is it loaded?" asked one of the new boys.

"Not that I know of," the fellow replied. There was a sudden bang and a bullet entered Harry's leg at the knee and exited at the ankle, hitting, but not severing, the sciatic nerve.

Harry was rushed to Holy Cross Hospital and promptly patched up. That night, a jubilant platoon of new recruits came to visit him. They dashed into the ward like madmen, waving newspapers in the air. There on the front page was the headline: "Harry Holmes, First Casualty in the 31st Battalion."

After a good laugh we concluded our car deal on the old parade grounds. This time the casualty was our pocketbook.

One time, Harry and I both were threatened with a gun. We were involved in a bank holdup, long before they became as fashionable as they are today.

One sunny winter afternoon Harry and I were taking our daily constitutional. As we passed the local shopping centre, I remembered an unpaid bill in my purse. It was just before three, so I rapidly steered Harry, white cane in his hand, through the doors of the bank.

As we stood at the customer service desk I heard a teller in a cheery voice say, "Hello, has it turned much cooler suddenly?" I looked up to see her serving a man in a tuque and a muffler that was pulled so far over his face he could hardly see.

"Shut up," the man replied, "and hand over your cash."

I thought it was a film and looked around for the cameras.

The teller shovelled over the money and promptly passed out. But she'd obviously had the presence of mind to press the alarm button, for the manager, eyes bulging, erupted from his office like a volcano.

Harry was completely oblivious of all the commotion. I was trying to fill him in in a whisper while exhorting him to keep still and not provoke the robber.

After stuffing the money into a bag, the robber turned on his heels and headed for the north door, but the manager got there first, snapped the lock and stood in front, wildly brandishing what looked like a revolver.

Turning swiftly on his heels, the robber headed back toward the south door we had entered. By this time the snow on his boots was beginning to melt and the water on the floor hampered his progress a little. He slipped around on the polished floor, coming very close to where we were standing.

I was terrified a shoot-out would start, and we would be caught in the cross fire.

"Stop that man," yelled the manager as the robber careered passed us.

Well, I'm sorry! But one of the reasons I've lived to a ripe old age is because I had no intention of trying to stop a young maniac with a gun.

Just as the robber arrived at the south door, in rushed a breathless customer, obviously relieved to find the bank still open. She smiled happily at the bank robber and held the door open for him as he rushed out.

I thought the manager would have apoplexy.

"I wish I knew what was going on," said Harry wistfully as we all stood in stunned silence.

Two policemen arrived and took statements. They seemed pleased that I could give a fairly good description of the robber and his outlandish garb. Harry was secretly delighted to be mixed up with crime again. He approved of the way I'd given a concise statement.

As we left the bank I realized I was carrying a news card from the local radio station. The station's telephone number was printed on the card, the idea being that any citizen who happened upon a good news story would phone it in. There was a prize for the best story of the month.

This was too good a chance to miss, so we rushed home and phoned CHED. The newsroom was delighted with the story and I found myself the winner of twenty-five dollars.

Once again, for us crime did pay.

The next morning we were startled to see two large men, one carrying a suitcase, approaching our front door. They identified themselves as plain-clothes detectives who needed my help.

I was puzzled until they opened the suitcase and pulled out a winter coat, muffler and tuque. "Do you recognize these?" they asked.

Indeed I did. They were the clothes the robber had worn. It seems he had stolen a car and then abandoned it, leaving his outer clothes under the seat. The detectives told me he had escaped with more than three thousand dollars. Not a bad haul for five minutes' work.

By this time the police and I were firm friends, and while I made them a cup of tea one started wandering around, looking at a couple of paintings on the wall.

"Who did these?" he asked.

Modestly I said I was the artist. This gave him a bright idea. "Say, could you sketch the holdup man?"

I wasn't sure how a sketch of a muffler and tuque was going to help, but at least I could give some idea of the general height and build.

The police were delighted and eventually left with my sketch in their files.

I felt we had survived this situation very well. We'd received a cheque for twenty-five dollars and my drawing hung in the rogues' gallery.

We dined out several times on this story but I had to stop telling it when I felt it was having an unsettling effect on our acquaintances. Not long after the incident, my old friend Rose Gallagher decided to find out for herself what really happens in holdups.

Eighty-year-old Rose was standing by her bank counter, fiddling in her capacious bag for her passbook. Instead of producing it she succumbed to a freakish impulse and quickly covered her hand with a scarf and stuck out two fingers. Then she pointed this gun shape at the teller and said, "Stick 'em up."

The teller pressed the alarm button and Rose calmly folded up her scarf and waited to see what would happen next.

The police arrived and were nonplussed to find a tiny white-haired old lady who smiled sweetly and said, "I'm sorry, my dears. I didn't want to cause any trouble. I just had the urge to see what would happen."

Obviously, news headlines flashed through he minds of the policemen: "Police Arrest 83-Year-Old Lady. Holds Up Bank With Her Finger."

They gave her a severe talking-to and she promised never to do it again.

34
The State Of The Art

The interest the police had shown in my paintings gave my morale a real boost. I had started painting as a retirement hobby several years before, having left my sixtieth birthday somewhere along the rocky road of life.

As always it was all systems go when I decided to try this new hobby. An eminent artist had promised me, "You'll never be the same again. A new world will open up for you." Naturally, I expected great things from my first class.

A friend, Gladys MacPherson, coaxed me into joining her on the new venture. She was going to take advantage of free art lessons for seniors and wanted a companion.

The "free" part appealed to my Yorkshire blood, and the "art" part sounded fun. I had a vision of myself with smock and palette, whipping up oils frantically.

What a letdown. When Gladys and I arrived for our first lesson, we found the class had been in progress for five weeks. Everyone was busy painting away, and to my inexperienced eye they all seemed to know their stuff. We were real beginners.

Diane, the teacher, settled us at an easel and presented us with our first subject: a couple of empty bottles and a lump of grubby material. She called this, still life. I thought it looked very dead, but struggled to try to capture its likeness with paper and charcoal. The resulting mess was pathetic.

At my side, Gladys was battling with her bottles. The results were similar to mine; a lot of black dust and smudges that in no way could be called art. The other students and the teacher were very polite, but as we left that first lesson we knew we were misfits, and our first thought was to quit.

After talking it over, we changed our minds. Neither of us had ever been quitters; in fact, we hated to be beaten. We would carry on. After all, painting is supposed to be therapeutic and calming for the *artist's* nerves. I'm not sure what it's supposed to do for the viewer.

Gladys and I persevered for several weeks and continued to make some interesting messes. Then Diane announced we were going to have a class show. I looked at my efforts and decided I didn't really want people to know who was responsible, so instead of signing them the usual way I signed my name backwards: Semloh.

Touring the exhibit during the show I overheard a remark. "Look at those," said a visitor, pointing to my work. "You know, he's that fellow from Yugoslavia. Quite remarkable, don't you think?"

We persisted with the class and turned out several credible efforts from the Chocolate Boxtop School of Art. Then Diane dropped a bombshell. "I'd like you to try some modern art."

The seniors all groaned loudly in chorus, but we went along with her request. I was in a fog about just how to proceed when I heard Diane say, "Remember, you are not painting what you see, but the cosmos around you."

That did it. I suddenly saw what she was getting at. From that moment on I was an abstractionist.

Life never was the same again. I had found my forte. I splashed around feverishly; the bigger the better, as far as I was concerned. Our house started to resemble a bohemian garret as I moved furniture out of the way to accommodate my easels.

Some of my paintings rather startled me, and I am sure they terrified the general public. Despite this they began to sell. A number of pictures were bought off my easel before the paint had even dried.

Often my inspiration would come at midnight. I would prop a canvas up on the mantelpiece and dabble around until the early hours of the morning. My paintings alternated between the normal and the distinctly abnormal. I was quite prolific and always experimented with new techniques. Harry was never sure what he would wake up to.

I had almost completed one abstract that was actually a collage of all kinds of interesting odds and sods applied to a canvas. It needed a very shiny varnish to bring out the highlights, so I whisked down to the marine supply store and came home with a bottle of polyurethane. That night I had a touch of nocturnal inspiration and dashed down to a small room in the basement, lit the gas fire, and began to smother my abstract in a coat of varnish.

I had no idea this varnish gave off toxic fumes, and as I worked I felt myself drifting off into another dimension. I put the effect down to true artistic euphoria, but gradually I realized that although the daze was very pleasant I was on the verge of passing out. I managed to drag myself up the stairs, open the back door, and thankfully gulp great draughts of fresh air.

I later used this varnish again, but always out in the garden. It gave excellent results, though never quite as spectacular as the first time.

Someone suggested I should become a member of the Edmonton Art Club. To achieve this kind of eminence you had to produce a number of paintings and be voted in.

The night of my audition it was forty below zero, with a horrendous wind. The gallery was in the Secord House, a historic building in the older part of town. We had set out early to allow lots of time to battle the elements, and arrived on the dot.

Harry and I began to unload my enormous paintings. By the time we had struggled both with pictures and wind we were exhausted. We clambered up the steps and rang the doorbell, only to discover we were the first ones there.

Harry and I stood on the steps with the wind catching the paintings and whipping them around like the sails of a clipper ship. Every minute I expected one of us to go bowling off down the road, or a painting to be ripped out of our frozen fingers.

167

Eventually we were let in. The paintings were confiscated and carried off up the old staircase. We had to await the verdict in the draughty old hall, like prisoners in dock.

One by one the jury crept back down the stairs with carefully schooled impassive expressions on their faces. Sometime later the foreman, with a very grim face, said, "They found your work very interesting, but you need more experience."

One or two of the more friendly artists tried to console me. "We voted for you," they said, as we trundled my offerings back to the car.

As I turned on the ignition and thankfully felt the car heater begin to work, an artist waved from the doorway. "Come and try again later," he called.

"Not on your nelly," I thought, as we drove off through the blizzard.

Despite this experience it wasn't long before I felt I had really arrived in the art world. One of my paintings was stolen from a gallery. The owner couldn't understand why I wasn't terribly upset, but I thought it was a wonderful compliment.

Deprived of the Art Club gallery in which to exhibit, I decided to turn my house into an art gallery. I hung my paintings all over the walls of the hallway and living room, and down the staircase into the basement.

Not long after I had finished this redecorating a fireman called in on one of Edmonton's fire-hazard spot checks. I was terrified of him seeing our basement; paints, turps and linseed oil were scattered all over the place.

I needn't have worried. He fell for one of my paintings on his way down the stairs and we completed the sale immediately. He walked off proudly with a painting under his arm, and my basement door stayed closed.

My next victim was the gas man. He came to read the meter, but being a navy man fell for some sailing ships I was working on.

I had many commissions in the fifteen years I painted, but none quite as strange as the one for my dear Aunt Nelly.

Harry and I had visited the old country again and I was looking forward to a long relaxing holiday. Unfortunately Aunt Nelly had other ideas. She had been intrigued with our letters describing my artistic endeavors and was determined to have a Semloh original.

She pounced on me as soon as we arrived, dragged me out into the back garden and pointed to the garage wall.

"I've had that wall sanded, scraped and painted white, ready for you to paint a mural on it," Aunt Nelly announced, explaining that she liked to sit at her window each day, looking out across the garden and onto the garage wall. "You choose your subject," Auntie said, "and I'll be able to think of you when you are back in Canada."

I'd done some pretty big paintings, but nothing of these dimensions. A mural on the side of the garage was the absolute limit.

There I was, expecting a restful holiday and faced with ladders, planks and boxes of painting supplies. My dreams of sunbathing on the beach were shot.

The next morning I buckled to and sketched a pleasing design of Monterey pines leaning over a cliff. These were among my favorite subjects, ever since I had first seen them growing precariously out of the rocks along the Oregon coast.

Aunt Nelly approved of the sketch, thank goodness, so I set up a sturdy arrangement of ladders and planks and attacked the wide expanse of wall.

England is not particularly well known for its wonderful summer weather and I thought I might get a few days rest when it rained. Unfortunately that was the summer it was so hot that water was rationed and the Thames was reputed to have dried up at its source.

I reeled around under blazing skies like a drunken sign painter. Each night, dizzy and exhausted, I rolled wearily into bed only to rise the next day and tackle another interminable stretch of boards.

My morale was not improved by a constant stream of northern relatives who kept popping in to eye the project with suspicion. Their Yorkshire wit did not strike me as very funny at the time and when one of them loudly asked my aunt, "Do they always do this kind of stuff in Canada?" he very nearly got a paint pot on his bald pate.

I did manage to finish the project, only to be promptly hospitalized with a bad case of sunstroke and shingles. Now I know how Michelangelo felt when he'd completed the ceiling of the Sistine Chapel: rotten.

What a way to spend a holiday! Many years later we made another trip to England and found out that my mural had stood up well to the rigors of the British climate. So had my Aunt Nelly.

While painting was my personal retirement hobby, Harry and I had a joint hobby that was giving us great pleasure: our grandchildren.

We rarely saw our grandchildren when they were not wet. Cheryl and Brenda had started swimming at a very early age and it quickly became apparent that young Brenda was not just good, she had championship promise.

Our lives often revolved around swim meets, and Harry and I enjoyed travelling around Alberta to watch Brenda swim competitively and the rest of the family work poolside — coaching, timing and helping with the many other jobs needed to run the meets.

After winning dozens of ribbons, Brenda started to bring home cups. The result was a roomful of trophies. Her dedication to the sport paid off when she was chosen to join the Canadian team at the 1972 Munich Olympics. At age fourteen she was the youngest competitor.

We were all so proud of her.

Bryan had arranged for Brenda to phone him from Munich and we gathered at his house at the agreed time, anxious to hear the results of her swim. He was staggered when upon our answering the phone she said, "Don't worry, they're taking care of us." Bryan, picking up the panic in her voice, carefully questioned her, and discovered that across the street from her balcony members of the Israeli team were being massacred.

Bryan immediately phoned the radio stations for more details, only to discover the news had not yet broken and his telephone call was one of the first leads to the story. This terrible incident destroyed the confidence of many young athletes and took all the joy out of the remaining events.

Brenda swam internationally for several years, completing her swimming career at the Commonwealth Games at Christchurch,

New Zealand.

Seeing so much water over these years, I never fancied getting into watercolors. Besides, as a true Albertan my medium was oil. During these years of splashing around I completed more than three hundred paintings.

Eventually I was actually asked to join the Edmonton Art Club, but Semloh had just sighted a new challenge. The city was offering some more free classes for seniors — this time in creative writing.

35
In My Own Write

Once again I found myself driving down a snowy street to an unknown class at the Senior Citizens' Recreation Centre. In my wildest imagination I would never have guessed that this was to be one of the turning points of my life.

There I was, seventy-four years old, and other than being an avid letter writer I'd no idea how to tackle "creative writing." Indeed I wasn't even quite sure what the term meant.

Walking into a strange class always takes courage, and once again everyone else seemed to know exactly what he or she was doing. This time, however, remembering my feelings of inadequacy during my first art class, I decided not to let my inexperience depress me.

I plunked myself firmly down on the nearest chair, drew a pencil and pad from my handbag, and tried my best to look intelligent. A pleasant-looking woman a couple of spaces away leaned over and addressed me in whisper. "Excuse me, but do you have a degree?"

"No," I replied, somewhat baffled.

She heaved a sigh of relief. "Thank heavens. Neither have I.

Come and sit by me."

And so I found my first friend in the world of writing.

We were lucky. The teacher, Elsie Park Gowan, was a woman after my own heart. She led us through the mysterious world of dangling participles and split infinitives with straightforward common sense. "Don't waste your time," she advised us. "Write about things you know."

This down-to-earth approach gave me great confidence, for I admired all the other writers in the class and knew I was starting with a disadvantage. Most had received a better education than my hit-and-miss affair, but maybe I could write about things that had happened to me.

Both Harry and Elsie encouraged me to overcome my fear that people wouldn't find my stories important. Each time I wrote an episode Harry would listen patiently and offer gentle criticism before I took it into the next class.

"You're a rotten speller and you cannot punctuate for nuts," he would tell me. "But keep on writing. You have a natural feel for a story and a lot of creative ability. After all, look at Churchill. He couldn't spell."

"Churchill had a full-time secretary," I'd grumble. And Harry would smile quietly, pick up my story and correct it.

Plodding on bit by bit I continued taking classes, working patiently on the exercises Elsie and other teachers gave us. I continued to write about the things I knew best: the days on the homestead, my childhood in Hull, and tales about the interesting people I'd met.

When looking through my work after several years of scribbling, I realized that I had accumulated nineteen episodes about our pioneering days, so I bundled them together and gave them to Elsie for some feedback. The following week she stomped into the class with my scribblings under her arm and dramatically thumped them down on the desk. "Do something with these!" she thundered.

That was all very well, but I was too startled to come back with, "What do you suggest?" So I gathered up the pages and took them home to think about.

Harry was thrilled with Elsie's reaction, but I confessed that I wasn't sure what to do next. We were both avid readers and knew that my little episodes were far too short to go into a book. Then Harry had a brainwave. "Do you think the CBC would be interested?"

At this time Harry was eighty-seven and his years were telling on him. His sight had deteriorated to the point he could only see things close up and in a good light, and he carried his white cane whenever we went out. He was also carrying around a large piece of shrapnel, a souvenir from World War One, and this was beginning to trouble him.

It was a major task to get Harry out at all, but we made the effort and he came with me to my classes. We always found willing volunteers to help him with coffee and sit and chat while I was busy. The idea of approaching the CBC, however, was a different proposition. The studios were far across the city; and even if we made the trip, nobody there would have the patience to read my sprawling handwriting. There seemed no point going.

Chatting with one of the class members, Rikki Salmon, I told her about the CBC idea. "I'll help you," she offered, and took my stories and neatly typed them up. This was the boost we needed. As soon as the pages were back in my hands, Harry and I bundled up and sallied forth in our little Datsun, across the city to the CBC.

The receptionist was far too well trained to look at all dismayed as we approached the desk. We certainly didn't look like the usual CBC clients. Harry was stooped over his white cane and leaning heavily on me, and I was too flustered from the effort of hauling him out of the car, to be able to speak immediately. We tottered across the interminable foyer and leaned against the desk to catch our breath. Harry, who always had a wicked sense of humor, whispered, "All we need is a little dog and a tin can and we've got it made."

The receptionist, Gerrie, greeted us kindly and listened patiently while I explained that I would like to show someone my stories. We were introduced to a very kind producer, Jackie Rollans, who promised to look over my material.

True to her word, a couple of weeks later Jackie Rollans phoned and asked if I would come down again to the CBC. She liked my style and wondered if I could write scripts.

Scripts? I'd never heard of them, but Jackie assured me she would be able to show me some samples.

I was shown how to dissect my stories and put them together as five-minute scripts. I had one question. "Do they all have to be homestead scripts?" I thought I would soon have that old homestead cow milked dry, and much to my relief I was told that I could also write the stories of interesting seniors.

Returning to Jackie with seven examples of radio scripts I found myself ushered into a studio.

"Have you ever used a mike?" I was asked as they stuck one in front of my face. I gathered I was about to be auditioned.

Who says you can't teach an old dog new tricks?

Everyone seemed surprised I wasn't nervous but I couldn't understand the fuss, and in no time we had recorded one of my scripts for the staff to listen to. Jackie seemed delighted. "You're a natural," she said.

"A natural what?" I wondered, remembering the twelve years of voice placement I'd taken with Madame Nurkse.

To my utter amazement, a job was offered. Would I like to do a spot on the early morning radio show, five days a week? At seventy-seven years of age I was embarking on a new career. I even had a theme tune. Thank heavens it wasn't Silver Threads among the Gold or The Old Grey Mare.

This Cinderella story is so unlikely, I still find it hard to believe the events — a matter of lucky timing — really happened.

After years of being relegated to the armchair, Senior Citizens were beginning to emerge as a group to be taken seriously. Realizing seniors were an untapped radio audience, the CBC was delighted when I walked in out of the blue with my pioneering stories. They were just the sort of tales to appeal to older people, many of whom had experienced similar events.

Who could have foreseen that my timid enquiries would produce such dramatic results?

Soon I became known as "a voice." After a couple of years a face was put to the voice when I appeared on several TV shows. I also became a much-requested public speaker.

I noticed that everyone I worked with had a fancy degree and

174

decided it was time to award myself one, too. I christened myself a D.O.P.E. — Doctor of personal experiences — and found that it really boosted my morale when I was asked to speak at universities and colleges. I always opened by announcing my degree, and once I had them laughing I could face my audience without a qualm.

Despite my busy schedule of driving to the CBC twice a week and conducting interviews, I managed to bathe Harry's legs and massage him several times a day. I had to do this constantly in order to keep him mobile enough to come with me. He loved our trips to the CBC. By now he was unable to read his beloved books and the radio was his great solace. He became a well-known figure at the studios, and anyone seeing him on his own would stop and chat and fill him in on some good stories.

Harry was my sounding board and listened several times to every script I wrote. First he would listen for dates and times. His memory was excellent and his court training made him very particular about accuracy. Then we would go over the script again and add more humor.

Rikki Salmon had made a wonderful contribution to my new career by typing my scripts, but I couldn't keep asking her to help — I was producing material far too fast. Harry came up with the solution. He dug out his old court typewriter, blew off the dust, explained its innards, and I learned to hunt and peck.

My first year of broadcasting was hectic but we revelled in our glimpses into a new and frantic world. Little did I realize it would be the last year of our life together.

The winter of 1975 became a real burden to Harry. He developed respiratory problems that eventually necessitated our having a large oxygen tank placed permanently between our beds.

Many a night I leaped out of bed and turned on the dials. We had a few close calls and several rushes to the hospital, but we managed to keep going until the spring. With the return of the daffodils, and the visits of a young rabbit that Harry fed every day on our front lawn, our spirits and his health began to pick up.

I tried to get ahead of schedule with my scripts and "put them in the can" as the broadcasting jargon says, for I never knew when we would next be rushing to the hospital.

Eventually, toward the end of a lovely May, Harry was rushed to the hospital for the last time. We suffered through ten anxious days when he was in a lot of pain. Then he died quietly one night, just before our sixtieth wedding anniversary.

During that first overwhelming grief I suddenly realized I should be on the air. I immediately phoned the CBC people to ask them to please take me off the program. This they did, and I was touched when they used my time slot for a moving memorial to Harry.

The next few weeks were very difficult despite my realization that we were lucky Harry had not spent too long lingering in the hospital. But the hard winter of nursing had taken its toll, and I was very tired. How grateful I was for the support of my family, my many friends and the CBC.

Bryan attended to all the funeral arrangements and, because Harry had been a lifelong member of the Canadian Legion, arranged an escort of their guard of honor. The coffin was covered with the flag.

The chapel was filled with our friends, and the floral tributes would have delighted Harry. I picked great bunches of his beloved white peonies and decorated our house and his coffin with them, both as a farewell and to show him I understood his view of death. To him it was a graduation from one life to another.

After the funeral, as I entered our house and looked at a vase full of these wonderful blooms, a petal detached itself and slowly dropped to the table. My eyes were dry for all my tears had been shed, but my heart ached and words and memories crowded in on me. I sat down and wrote a poem.

The petal falls from the peony:
Memories float through my mind.
Life is beautiful.
Highs and lows, loves ever mine.
The funeral flowers are fresh and brave
Then: The petal falls from the peony.

36
On My Own

I never understood why Greta Garbo had always wanted to be alone. I hated it. I had no choice in the matter, however, and had to accept my fate.

My many personal friends and my listening audience, who also felt they knew me, were incredibly understanding, but I knew that to give way to grief completely was not a good idea.

I did my best to keep the CBC schedule, and I was heart-warmed by the flood of supportive messages, many from complete strangers who felt they knew Harry from my pioneer stories. This response comforted me and helped me through many lonely moments, but it posed me with a problem. Good manners dictated I should answer all the letters, yet there were so many I wasn't sure where to start.

Again my lucky star was on the horizon. Gladys MacPherson, my old friend from the art class, was in Edmonton on a visit from the coast. She phoned and asked if I would like her to stay an extra week so she could act as my personal secretary and help with the mail.

What a terrific boost to my recovery. Gladys provided someone to talk to and took away the guilt I was feeling about the piled-up letters.

I gradually began to pick up the pieces of my life and put them together in a different pattern. I refused to take any medication from the doctor, for I knew that grieving was a healing process and had to be done naturally. Besides, I needed all my wits about me to make the many decisions ahead.

Some years previously, Harry and I had sold our house and moved into a senior citizens' housing complex for married couples. We had been extremely happy with the move, but during this period the one enormous drawback of the complex became apparent. The week following Harry's death I received notice to quit the house within three months; the apartments were for married couples only! This was a double blow. Losing your spouse means a heart-breaking adjustment. To lose your home at the same time seems cruel.

Adaptability must be my middle name. I decided to tackle the problem head on, so applied for an apartment in the new senior citizens' high rise being constructed on the south side of Edmonton.

As soon as my present complex heard I was on the Strathcona Residence waiting list, I was given permission to stay where I was until the new apartment was ready.

Hurray. A major problem surmounted.

I thanked my stars for the broadcasting commitments. They forced me to keep going and meet a steady schedule on those terrible days when I would have loved to stay in bed and cry.

Often I had to force myself to get up and face the world. Then I would find the day was over; I'd been so busy I had no time to be sorry for myself. I worked hard and managed to get some extra scripts in the can. Finally, toward the end of the summer, I was free to take a much-needed break and visit my beloved ocean. My grief was still there, but the threads of my life were beginning to pull together again and I was learning to do things on my own.

My desire to visit the coast coincided with an invitation from young friends living in Powell River, north of Vancouver. They had built a boat and were planning a launching ceremony. Would I like to attend?

This sounded like fun, and just what I needed.

Gerry Bennett had always wanted a boat, so he finally decided to build one as a winter project. For months it graced his basement and his friends were looking forward to the day it would receive the final touches and take its rightful place on the ocean. Unfortunately, no one had measured the basement opening before construction. The air was blue when Gerry and friends realized they would have to remove the basement wall to get the boat out.

I refrained from asking details about how this task was finally achieved, but achieved it was. The boat, a lovely piece of work, greeted me upon my arrival. It sat proudly in the middle of the front lawn, its paint gleaming in the sunshine, ready for the big moment.

Gerry and a couple of friends carefully carried the boat down to the sea for its maiden voyage. Other friends followed behind, stopping at the liquor store to purchase the traditional bottle.

Irish Mist was selected as the most appropriate libation, and with a great flourish Gerry presented the bottle to a teaching colleague who flexed her muscles ready to do the honors.

To my astonishment a cassette tape recorder was produced, and to start the ceremony the music of the Coldstream Guards, playing a rousing traditional march, smote our ears.

As the strains echoed across the harbor a few curious neighbors gathered to swell the admiring audience. By the time the guards changed their tune to Anchors Away, a few of Gerry's young students appeared to cheer us on.

The young woman stepped forward to play her part. The audience was dumbfounded when she took a deep breath and perfectly imitated the voice of Queen Elizabeth.

"My husband and I, on this suspicious occasion, take great pleasure in presenting Commander Gerry Bennett with the order of the bath in recognition of his devotion in maintaining the traditions of the Empire in its farflung corners."

Gerry stood before her, head bowed, while she graciously draped his chest with a ribbon and a bath plug.

The boat was then ceremoniously pushed into the water.

At this point the proceedings deviated drastically from the norm. "Seems a pity to waste all this," said the queen, and she passed the bottle around for a quick swig.

As soon as the empty bottle returned to her hands, we continued. "It gives me great pleasure to name this boat Irish Mist, and may God help all who sail in her."

As the crowd cheered, sirens sounded and the Coldstream Guards roared, the Commander leapt into his boat ready to steer it, and the queen whacked the empty bottle across the bows.

The wind filled the sails, and the little boat gently heeled to one side and then, with a big lurch, keeled completely over.

The commander, laughing uncontrollably, clung to the side of his bobbing craft as water bubbled up through the unfilled bungholes.

The queen, never at a loss for words, yelled, "shove in the plug and I'll launch this pesky boat again."

Laughter has always been the best medicine and this crazy interlude at the coast was just what was needed to set me, if not the boat, on an even keel. I came back to Edmonton still grieving, but rested and ready to start my new life.

As usual the mail had piled high while I was away, and among the many letters was a notice giving me a date for moving into the senior citizens' high rise. The city had allotted me an apartment on the fifth floor; I was about to reside in a room with a view.

I visited the new apartment several times with a number of friends. We all liked its big windows and light-colored walls that gave the illusion of more space than was actually there, and everyone gave me ideas about how I could arrange my furniture to best advantage.

It is always difficult to move to a smaller house. The very things I wanted to take for sentimental reasons were the pieces that didn't fit. My favorite chairs seemed too big and clumsy for a small room, and the old-fashioned oak desk that we'd had for years seemed likely to overpower the place.

I was in despair. How could I pick and choose and decide what to leave behind?

Eventually Andrea, a young friend, came to my rescue. She and her family had just moved to a new house and were used to working out such wrinkles. Armed with a tape, Andrea measured all the furniture. Then we went to the high rise and took all the vital statistics there. It was amazing how everything fell into place when I wasn't guessing any more.

The next step was to book a moving van. I looked in the Yellow Pages and boggled at the list. All the ads looked the same to me so I plumped for one with a name that appealed: The Big Four. Envisioning the four husky men who presumably did the job, I booked them and felt really organized. By this time I could view the whole upheaval with confidence, and despite all the changes I was able to cope.

Friends and family kept appearing to help and transport my small things so that moving day would not be a big job. They were so efficient that the week before the actual move, I woke

180

one morning to the realization that the only things left to go were my bed and clothes. There didn't seem much point in having The Big Four for a single bed.

Moving was a painless and inexpensive experience, costing me only a few cases of beer for the willing helpers. And there I was, now safely ensconced in a high-rise apartment with whirlpool bath, party room, games room and library. I considered myself very fortunate.

During this period I didn't miss a beat with my CBC work. My pioneer reminiscences were a little too close to home to broadcast, but my producer gave me permission to choose whatever I liked, and I flung myself into interviewing other oldtimers and broadcasting their stories. I kept up my schedule of five scripts a week and I met some wonderful people.

Suitable subjects were found everywhere — sitting next to me on a park bench, waiting at a bus stop, shopping in the mall; in fact, anywhere there were people. My approach was subtle. I'd just ask them where they came from and what they did and the stories spilled out. It seemed as though everybody had a story, but no one had ever asked about it. I rarely had to ask more than one leading question for most of my victims to be cooperative.

One time, I was given a most interesting story on the early days of coal mining, but my subject refused to let me use his name on the air. When I asked why he replied, "My wife will give me hell." I suggested it would be possible to change any names in the story, including his own. Then he gave permission, as long as I called him James McFadden.

I was attending a party several months after the coal mining story had been aired, and a woman approached me.

"Excuse me, but are you Peggy Holmes?"

"Yes, I am."

"Do you remember the coal mining story about the explosion in the Crowsnest Pass?"

"Yes," I replied warily.

"Well, I was the secretary and bookkeeper at the Crowsnest Mine. I remember that explosion clearly, but you've got me flummoxed. I don't remember a James McFadden working there. I phoned the mine manager; he'd also heard your broadcast and wondered about the same thing. The story was correct in every detail except for the name of the worker."

At this point I made a fatal mistake. I explained that I had been asked to keep the name secret.

"Could I ask why the worker wanted to remain anonymous?"

"He said his wife would give him hell."

The lady burst out laughing. "I know exactly who that worker is."

Moral: Never explain your reasons. Just look blank.

I've learned a lot about interviews since those early days and have managed to avoid similar situations. Later on I graduated from interviewing pioneers to interviewing as well some of the top theatre personalities who were passing through Edmonton.

One of my favorite people was David Langton, known to so many fans as Lord Bellamy from Upstairs Downstairs.

Arriving at the fancy apartment block where he was staying, I buzzed his door and was quite surprised when his mellow voice answered. He met me as I stepped off the elevator and I explained I had quite expected Hudson to receive me. This really broke the ice and I found him and his wife delightful and refreshingly relaxed.

During the interview he jumped up. "Excuse me a minute, Peggy, I have to do the spuds." Obviously working with Mrs. Bridges and Hudson had not given him ideas above his station.

David told me some very funny stories about the TV series and we discussed all the beautiful wives he married as Lord Bellamy. Looking across the room at his real wife, I realized none of them could hold a candle to her. He told me that the writers had to drown Lady Marjorie, as she'd been offered another assignment.

I enjoyed visiting the Langtons so much that I asked David if he and his wife would like to come to my senior citizens' residence.

"Certainly," replied David. "I do a lot of charity work."

"Charity nothing," I screamed. "I'm inviting you for lunch."

David graciously accepted and I arranged to have them picked up the following day.

Unfortunately the CBC newsman who was to pick them up

was detained on a critical assignment, which left my elderly Datsun as the sole means of transportation. Now I realize this doesn't sound like the end of the world, but it was forty below and blowing a blizzard, and there was not a cab to be had anywhere.

It took me a long time to battle the weather and chaotic traffic, but eventually I arrived to find David waiting for me outside. He was dressed in a thin English trench coat and his ears were a fine shade of blue. Thank heavens my little Datsun, though far from the most elegant transportation in the world, had a good heater.

Rushing inside he summoned his wife, and she materialized in a long, cream-colored mink coat. Somehow I crammed them in my car hoping that no black marks would smudge the mink, which I assume cost more than all the cars I have ever owned.

Gingerly we inched our way over the icy roads, heaving a united sigh of relief when we arrived safely at the door of my building. We had a hearty meal, and David gradually thawed out.

I was amused at the number of people who thought they knew David but couldn't place him.

It was during this period that Joy Roberts came into my life. She phone me one day, saying, "Peggy, you don't know me, but I hear you would like to collaborate with someone to compile your pioneer stories into a book."

Joy Roberts was correct. I did need help in compiling a full-length book. I was so used to writing five-minute scripts it was hard to think in terms of a long manuscript. I was ready and willing to take up a new challenge if someone could offer help and expertise.

Help was forthcoming. Joy arranged my many scribblings, completed the episodes and gave unstintingly of her advice. There was a tremendous amount of work for us both to do, but It Could Have Been Worse was completed early in 1978. In 1979 it won the Hudson's Bay Beaver Award for an unpublished manuscript and was then picked up by Collins for publication.

Despite Harry's death and the upheaval of changing the patterns of a lifetime, I was coming to terms with a solitary existence and had found a new outlet.

At the ripe old age of eighty-two, I was an author.

37
The Bull And I

At one time or another during a lifetime you are bound to be upstaged, but not many people are upstaged by a Brahma bull. This happened to me the night before my eighty-fifth birthday.

I'd been invited as a guest on Tommy Banks Live, a popular Alberta-based television variety and talk show. My birthday falls on November 11, Remembrance Day, and Tommy Banks asked me to reminisce about my twenty-first birthday. That traumatic day was the one so long ago when Harry and I learned the armistice had been signed, thus ending the hostilities of the first world war.

For some reason that still escapes me, Tommy had also invited a prize Brahma bull.

The bull was standing quite placidly when I first clapped eyes on him. "Hmm," I thought, "they're tempting providence. The bull's not going to like that strip of red carpet."

As if to agree with me, the bull lowered his head toward the carpet and sniffed suspiciously. Then I realized that I was wearing a bright red flowing dress. As I moved across the studio the bull turned his beady eye on me, and I wished I'd worn black.

For a bull he was remarkably tame. He ignored the lights and cameras with quiet disdain. I sat at the back of the studio, near the exit, and kept a firm eye on him until it was my turn for the limelight.

As I walked on the set, Tommy presented me with a beautiful bouquet of flowers, mostly red carnations. "Oops," said the little voice at the back of my head. "They are really trying to liven this show up."

The bull eyed my flowers with interest, but instead of looking fierce he seemed to have a dreamy look upon his face. I thought of Ferdinand, the bull who went to pieces at the sight of a flower, and I hoped this one would go weak at the knees until I got safely out of the studio. My eighty-five-year-old legs were all right for getting around as long as I wasn't expected to run.

The interview started out simply and staidly as I talked about my war experiences. Tommy Banks and the audience were very intent, but Mr. Bull seemed a little restless. Worried that he was still eyeing my flowers, I moved them to the other arm and half-turned so that they were out of his sight. This seemed to settle him, and he stood calmly. I felt as though I were sitting on a keg of dynamite. As each second ticked its way steadily to the end of the program, I was more certain something was going to happen.

Well, it did. But not quite the way I had imagined.

The bull never did rampage about, or even paw the ground and bellow. No. He waited until the program was almost finished, and then he copiously watered the carpet.

After the excitement of that night, waking up to my actual birthday was almost an anticlimax.

I have always viewed my birthday morning with mixed feelings. Remembrance Day is an emotional time for many people, and for me that first armistice day was the happiest day of my life. By the grace of God, Harry was saved at the last minute from going back to the trenches. But the day also brings sad memories.

I got up slowly and turned on the television. It was time to participate quietly in the Remembrance Day service and shed a few tears for Harry, his comrades, and all those unknown people who suffered or lost their lives during the wars.

How delighted I was when Andrea, one of my unofficially adopted family, came breezing in with a gift and cards drawn by her husband and children. "I've come to be with you for the service. We didn't want you to be on your own." Together we shared that solemn moment by sitting side by side holding hands.

Solemnity finished for the day, Andrea and I turned our attention to the forthcoming party, and I felt the excitement beginning to bubble inside me. I have always loved parties, and tonight Bryan was hosting a cheese and wine party for a few of my friends.

That was the original idea.

When Bryan asked for my guest list his eyebrows rose just like his father's. "Are *all* these people your friends?"

"Good heavens, not by any means. I couldn't possibly ask you to entertain more than the first hundred."

He looked bemused, but forbore from further comment. Then I had another idea.

"We'll be using the party room at my senior citizens' high rise, so why not have the cheese and wine for private guests from six o'clock to eight, and then open the room for a coffee party for everyone in the building?"

Bryan gave a sigh. Then the humor of the situation got to him and he burst out laughing. "You never did do things in small way, so I guess it's too late to ask you to now."

Early in the afternoon flowers began to arrive. There were so many of them and they were all so lavish I really began to wonder if I was featured in the obituary column by mistake. Still, I was glad I was alive and kicking to enjoy them.

Next came the champagne. For a quiet evening with a few friends, this was turning out to be quite a celebration.

The first guests arrived, and with them the entertainment. "Where do you want these instruments?"

Heavens, I didn't even know what the entertainment was to be, let alone where it should go. I pointed to the Master of Ceremonies, Doug Robb, another of my unofficial family.

The party room is very large, but it filled up rapidly. By the time I cut the birthday cake there were more than two hundred guests, and you could hardly move. Bryan had done a wonderful job of the catering, though, and like the proverbial loaves and fishes there was enough to go around. This didn't stop him from digging me in the ribs as we surveyed the crush.

"I love your idea of a few friends," he whispered.

By the time the entertainment commenced, every chair was filled and the rest of the crowd sat on the floor. What a show. I didn't realize just how many talented friends I'd made. Folk music, light opera and the musical hall — all were represented. Sandwiched in the middle was Alfred Hooke, a former Social Credit cabinet minister who convulsed us all by reciting Albert and the Lion, much to the delight of a present cabinet minister, the Honourable Horst Schmid.

The party drew to a rousing finale with an old-fashioned sing-along around the piano. Someone had deposited a bottle of champagne on the top, and it jigged around happily with the vibrations. Suddenly it exploded with a loud pop, and my party really did go off with a bang.

As the guests departed, hours after the planned ten o'clock, many of them complimented Bryan and asked if he was planning another party when I reached ninety.

He shook his head in a dazed fashion. "Not likely. Next time we're taking her to Hawaii."

As I look back over my years of wonderful friendships and adventures, I know I have been blessed. So many stories remain untold I already feel the need to start the next book. So far I have given you only the highlights; the real revelations are to come. But, if my time runs out, I'll just reincarnate to give you the rest.

"Why does everything happen to you, Peggy?" is a question I am often asked but have trouble answering.

Privately, I am of the opinion that these situations happen to everyone, but maybe I have an extra twist to my funny bone that allows me to see the ridiculous side of most incidents.

So, on to my next project.

I've just bought a harp. Living in a small apartment, the only place I have room to practise is the bathroom. Eyebrows are raised, but I don't understand why. After all, many people sing in the shower.

I practise most days and have even made my public debut. Andrea and her youngest daughter visited England for three weeks. Her husband Dave came with me to buy the harp, and he succumbed to the instrument he has always wanted to play, a violin. Dave and I practised frantically for the three weeks, and then met Andrea at the airport. As she walked through customs we serenaded her with There's No Place Like Home.

She was somewhat overcome. I hope it was with the right emotion.

I am trying to improve my playing, slowly and carefully. I don't want to be good enough to be called up to join the harp section of the heavenly choir.

Oh yes, the mail arrived this morning. It contained an interesting invitation. How would I like to go up in a hot air balloon? Now *there* is something I've always wanted to do...